THE PLAY'S THE THING

Four Original Television Dramas

THE PLAY'S THE THING

Four Original Television Dramas

Edited by
Tony Gifford
Utilization Officer
Educational Media Division
Ontario Educational Communications Authority

Macmillan of Canada

© 1976 The Macmillan Company of Canada Limited
70 Bond Street, Toronto M5B 1X3
Affiliated with Maclean-Hunter Learning Materials Company.

ISBN 0-7705-1291-7

Printed in Canada

Illustrations by Emma Hesse

Contents

Introduction

Drama on television differs from that in the theatre in many ways. The actor in the theatre has an audience that is present, whereas the television actor has to imagine and predict the audience's response. In television, the cameras enable the audience to see the actor at very close range, so that the softest whisper, or the slightest movement such as the flicker of an eyelid, can heighten the tension of a scene. In the theatre this kind of subtlety would not even be noticed. Acting on the stage, because of the distance between performer and audience, demands large, expressive gestures, and loud voices. In order to get the play's message across, the stage actor must work with his or her entire body.

When portraying outdoor scenes, the theatrical set has to suggest an external location, but the television set can actually be external.

Within a scene, television creates many points of view and angles of vision for the audience; the theatre can present only one point of view and one angle of vision.

The television cameras enable us to see, through the techniques of dissolving, fading, and cutting, many more things at the same time than are possible in the theatre.

"Drama ought to be the jewel in television's crown; the thing that sets standards for the rest of the industry to emulate," said Lee Strasberg, artistic director of the Actors' Studio. A theatre person for many years, Strasberg nevertheless believed "Television drama can be even better than theatre drama, because you can get the one performance you want. Television, like movies, has the one great capability that theatre doesn't have: you can freeze excellence. That's why creating plays for television requires a great responsibility. These are the documents upon which the history of our culture will be written."

The Canadian Broadcasting Corporation has for some time accepted such a responsibility and challenge for developing Canadian television drama. The television scripts in this anthology are from one of their most successful drama series called "The Play's the Thing". As part of their attempt to foster national culture, entertainment, and education, this series (which was televised from

September 1973 through May 1974) showcased Canadian writing, producing, directing, and acting of the highest calibre. Nationally acclaimed for their artistic and technical merit, the television dramas in "The Play's the Thing" were considered as excellent examples of craftsmanship, experimentation, and video technique.

The material written and developed for television drama comes from many sources: short stories, novels, art reproductions, historical documents, autobiographies, and theatre plays. Notice that many television dramas are adaptations from other forms of media; moreover, many of the original medium's forms as well as its content are adapted into television drama. Increasingly, however, television dramas are being written that are not adaptations but rather are original, and are oriented totally to television.

This anthology contains two television dramas adapted from short stories: Alice Munro's "How I Met My Husband" and Hugh Hood's "Friends and Relations". We have included Hugh Hood's original short story so that you can explore how one author adapted a prose work for television. The anthology also includes a documentary drama, "The Roncarelli Affair", which was created especially for television through the collaborative dramatization of Mavor Moore and F. R. Scott from Scott's personal records and reminiscences. Eric Nicol's television drama "The Man from Inner Space" is an original comedy script written expressly for television—it is difficult even to imagine this script being done in the theatre.

Hugh Hood's "Friends and Relations" portrays one woman's struggles to become independent and the shaper of her own destiny in a society that seems male-dominated. "How I Met My Husband" by Alice Munro examines some romantic and traditional ideas of women in order to analyse "the waiting game". We meet the satirical and comic vision of Eric Nicol in "The Man from Inner Space", which demonstrates that none can escape the absurd realities we love to hate. In "The Roncarelli Affair" by F. R. Scott and Mavor Moore, the harsh world of politics and the law makes a mockery of justice and mercy. All these television dramas, then, provide examples of personal dilemmas and social issues that relate to our lives. They offer us the opportunity to reflect upon those examples, to recognize analogies to our own experience, and to understand visually how they can affect what we do.

In reading, rather than watching, a television drama, you are cut off from the atmosphere and medium that make the drama live. You must play an active role yourself, substituting your imagination for the setting, technical effects, costumes, mood, and acting techniques. Pay close attention to the author's acting directions and technical notes. In your imagination, you can achieve all the effects you want.

It will be helpful to you to keep in mind the fantastically complex and collaborative effort behind any television drama. Many believe that only the actors are responsible for the merit of a television drama. But they are only the tip of the iceberg. They should be considered as only one part of the Production Team. Remember this team as you are analysing and experiencing these television dramas.

The Production Team

The Director
is in charge of the studio crew and all other components of the program. He will see that the studio is set with the aid of his floor crew and then from his position in the control room he shapes the program by watching his monitors, following the script, and directing the operations of switcher, cameras, and sound. He communicates with his crew members through an intercom headset.

The Switcher
selects the pictures the director chooses, balances the video, and makes the best picture possible.

The Audio Engineer
follows direction about the initiation, regulation, balance, and blend of all sound in the program.

The Script Assistant
is responsible for assembling the thoughts and the technical and acting notes of the team into a meaningful outline for the cast director and the crew to follow.

The Floor Manager
represents the director on the studio floor. He communicates with the director via his headset and is responsible for managing the performers, the cameramen, the sound (boom) man, the propmen, and the stagehands.

The Camera Operators
translate the director's instructions into pictures of good composition and clarity.

The Boom Operator
catches the sound with his long pole-like boom and microphone and is the audio engineer's floor assistant.

The Graphics and Props
people are responsible for the art cards, still pictures, and titles and credits, and for the operation of the graphics console, as well as for the organization of the props and costumes.

The Performers
are called "the talent" by those in the TV business. They complete the TV team. Much of their work—the rehearsing, the learning of lines, and the working out of the script—is done off camera.

This anthology's television dramas often include the camera positions and takes, together with the techniques of console switching. Sometimes they are written in a shorthand (CU for close-up). To help you visualize these scripts, remember the following terms. However, also remember that they are only one way (actually, that of the original production team) to visualize the script. Experiment with your own ways—a script is not law, but only a guide.

Some Television Terms

CLOSE-UP (CU)
Narrow-angle picture limited to object or part of object instead of scene. No background.

BIG CLOSE-UP or TIGHT CLOSE-UP (BCU or TCU)
Very narrow angle, usually just one feature of an object or subject so that it completely fills the frame with no extraneous material.

MEDIUM CLOSE-UP (MCU)
Medium-angle picture showing object and limited amount of background or setting.

MEDIUM SHOT (MS)
Wide angle showing objects and related material.

FULL SHOT or COVER SHOT (FS or CS)
Shot revealing all parts of objects mentioned.

LONG SHOT or ESTABLISHING SHOT (LS)

A full view in which figures or objects are smaller than frame and sensation of distance is achieved. Also used to establish the relationship of the people and objects in it to one another. Usually the scene opener.

TWO-SHOT (2-S)

Composition of two performers or objects.

THREE-SHOT (3-S)

Composition of three performers or objects.

DOLLY IN (DI)

Camera is moved toward talent for closer shot while on the air.

DOLLY BACK (DB)

The camera is moved back by cameraman or dolly man.

PAN RIGHT, PAN LEFT (PR-PL)

Camera is turned horizontally to right or left over a scene, set, or group, the cameraman keeping the people in focus.

TILT UP, TILT DOWN (TU-TD)

Camera is aimed up or down in a vertical plane, to show objects either above or below the action or scene. For instance, the height of a man can be established by first showing the viewers a close-up of the man's feet. Then, by tilting up (and dollying back slowly) the camera can show the manner and dress of the man, ending with a head-shot or close-up of his face.

DISSOLVE (DIS)

Bringing in one picture while dissolving out another; designates a short lapse of time, effects a smooth, restful, easy transition from one image to another, and is also used for dramatic effect as dissolving from a photographic slide to a performer in the studio, giving the effect of a photograph coming to life.

LAP DISSOLVE

Holding two cameras at half-lap, which means having the images taken by two cameras shown on the television screen at the same time. This technique is used for trick effects, for transitional effects, for montage effects, and for establishing locales.

FADE IN (FI)

Gradually bringing up a picture from black level. Indicates a definite beginning, such as the fading in of the title of a program and the fading in of the opening picture of a scene.

FADE OUT (FO)
Gradually dimming a picture, i.e., going to black level. Indicates a definite termination of chapter, scene, idea, or picture sequence. The last scene of a play or program is usually faded out.

CUT
Stop action, music, cameras, etc.

CUT TO
Switching direction from one camera picture to another. Indicates no lapse in time and usually speeds up action when used for dramatic impact.

EXTERNAL SEQUENCE (EXT.)
A sequence taken out of doors.

INTERNAL SEQUENCE (INT.)
A sequence taken indoors.

SEGUE
A fade from one audio source to another.

VOICE OVER
The voice of an actor or a narrator heard off camera describing actions or events that are shown on the television screen.

How I Met My Husband

Alice Munro

How I Met My Husband

Alice Munro

Characters

EDIE about 15 or 16, country-girl of the late 1940s, fairly pretty.

EDIE a grown woman. As narrator (voice over)

LORETTA BIRD countrywoman in her 30's, much deteriorated in appearance, slatternly clothes, great interest in other people's lives, malice so open it has a glow of innocence.

DR. PEEBLES veterinary surgeon, early 30's, agreeable, not perceptive.

MRS. PEEBLES early 30's, good-looking, mildly discontented, sharper than her husband.

CHRIS WATTERS good-looking, easily courteous, sometimes teasing, absolutely secretive, damaged, fleeing young man. He offers people his kindness, hoping they won't ask anything else. His flirtatiousness is responsive, even defensive. Women of course find him attractive.

ALICE KELLING about thirty, maybe a bit older, not very attractive but very tenacious. A recipient of Chris's kindness, a follower-up of flirtatiousness, perhaps at one time someone he needed, who refuses to let go.

MAILMAN shy, ordinary-looking young countryman.

JOEY 6 or 7 years old.

HEATHER 9 or 10 years old.

ACT ONE

FADE IN:

SCENE 1: EXTERNAL SEQUENCE. DAY. THE PEEBLESES'
YARD.

Edie, Joey, and Heather are picking berries along the roadside close
to a mailbox, on which is written: Dr. G. A. Peebles.

   SOUND *of approaching car. The children look up, run towards*
the mailbox, calling, "It's the mailman!", "Mailman's here!", or
something of that sort.

   Car slows, veers off the road, stops at the mailbox. The mailman
leans out and hands the mail to the children, dividing letters and
circulars so they both get some (meanwhile smiling uncertainly at
Edie, who has come up behind them, not too close).

Mailman: Get some berries?

Edie nods. They should both seem shy, though without particular
tension, when Edie speaks, it is as though curiosity, and perhaps
some homesickness, had got the better of her.

Edie: Are you a Carmichael?

Mailman: *(Pleased)* How come you knew that?

Edie: Your face.

Mailman: How come?

Edie: There's some Carmichaels living out by us.

Mailman: Don't you live here?

Edie: *(Shakes her head, indicating no dissatisfaction but perhaps*
   limitations.) Just work.

   The car pulls away. Edie carrying berry pail, follows the children
into the house.

DISSOLVE TO:

Edie's voice: *(This is the narrating voice of Edie as a mature*
   woman, just a little more grainy, confident, wry, than the voice
   of Edie as a girl.) I was fifteen and away from home for the first
   time. My parents had made the effort and sent me to high school

for a year but I didn't like it. Dr. Peebles was staying at our place for dinner, having just helped one our cows have twins, and he said I looked smart to him and his wife was looking for a girl to help.

CUT TO:

SCENE 2: INTERNAL SEQUENCE. DAY. THE PEEBLESES' KITCHEN.
Very up-to-date late 1940s.
Loretta Bird knocks, lets herself in, sits down at the table, concerned to make herself look at home, but obviously too avid and alert to be at home.
Edie washing dishes, mopping counters, polishing taps. All Edie's work is done with great care and pride, even delight.

Loretta: Has Dr. Peebles gone back to town? *(Edie nods or murmurs affirmatively.)* Veterinarians don't always get called Doctor. Some do, some don't. *(No comment from Edie. She should respond only when necessary, minimally, to all the following questions and comments.)* Is she taking her nap? *(Edie nods.)* She wouldn't find the time to lie down in the middle of the day if she had seven kids, like me. They sure fixed this place up. I can't understand why they wouldn't want to live in town.

Edie's voice: Loretta Bird lived next door and the Peebleses thought she was a countrywoman; they didn't know the difference. Her husband worked on the roads and had a bad name for drinking. The Peebleses always made her welcome.

Loretta: Do they ever have their disagreements? Him and her? *(Edie frowns: no comment.)* Do they keep any of them things in their bedside drawers? *(Edie looks surprised.)* Them things you keep from having babies with. *(Edie darkly embarrassed, resolutely unresponsive.)* Because if they do, it's a sin.

DISSOLVE TO:

SCENE 3: INTERNAL SEQUENCE. DAY. THE PEEBLESES' BATHROOM.
Pink fixtures and lights, soft, thick towels and mats, three-way mirror. The bathroom should look luxurious in a standard suburban 1940s–1950s style.
Steam rising. During the following scene Edie can stand on the

side of the tub, nude, to look at herself in the three-way mirror. Or draped in a towel, sliding it around to look like a sarong, if you prefer. She can make use of various big talcum puffs, spray colognes, she can slide back the glass shower-doors. She should admire herself, but mostly her surroundings. This can be shot as one bathroom scene, or a divided scene, with Edie first in the bathroom, then in the kitchen (dressed, at a different time), admiring the appliances, snapping on the fluorescent lights, looking in the refrigerator, etc.

Edie's voice: The Peebleses wouldn't have minded if I took a bath oftener than once a week. But I wouldn't take the risk of making it less wonderful.

   Sometimes I thought about the way we lived out home and the way they lived here and how one way was so hard to imagine when you were living the other way. But I thought it was still a lot easier, living the way we did at home, to picture something like this, than it was for anybody knowing only things like this to picture the other way.

DISSOLVE TO:

SCENE 4: INTERIOR SEQUENCE. DAY. THE PEEBLESES' DINING ROOM.

Edie's voice: Dr. and Mrs. Peebles were nice to me, as much as they could be. They had me eat my meals with them—to tell the truth I expected to, I didn't know there were families who don't.

During the last part of Edie's narration we see her approach the dining-room table at which Dr. and Mrs. Peebles, Joey, and Heather are seated. Edie carries a salad plate which she puts on the table, then seats herself.

Mrs. Peebles: *(Indicating dish)* I think my jellied salad turned out well. Have some.

Dr. Peebles: Very nice.

Joey: I want some pie.

We hear the SOUND *of a plane, growing louder.*

Dr. Peebles: Listen, what on earth . . .

Joey: A plane! A plane! It's gonna crash into the house . . . *(Joey jumps up and rushes out of the dining room, followed by the others.)*

CUT TO:

SCENE 5: EXTERNAL SEQUENCE. DAY. THE PEEBLESES' YARD.
They run into the yard, looking up, watching the plane come in over the tree-tops and land across the road, in the fairgrounds.

Joey: Is it gonna be a crash landing?

Dr. Peebles: Of course not. He knows what he's doing, Joey.

Mrs. Peebles: *(Relieved, after a moment's watching)* All right. Back in the house. Let's not stand here gawking like a set of farmers.

Guarded look on Edie's face. Loretta Bird comes around the corner of the house, out of breath.

Loretta: I thought he was going to kill youse all.
    I know what he's landed here for. I bet he's got permission to use the fairgrounds and take people up for rides. It's the same fellow who was over at Palmerston last week and was up the lakeshore week before that. I wouldn't go up if you paid me.

Dr. Peebles: I would. I'd like to see this neighbourhood from the air.

Mrs. Peebles: I can see all I need to see of it from the ground.

Heather: I want to go up in the plane! How about you, Edie?

Edie: I don't know.

Loretta: People are going to be coming out here in cars raising up dust and tramping on your property. If I was youse I would complain.

Mrs. Peebles: Will you have some dessert?

Loretta: Well, as long as it's not out of a tin. I haven't got the right kind of stomach for tins. I can only eat home canning.

Edie looks as though she could slap her. They all begin to move back into the house.
    The plane is sitting in the fairgrounds.

DISSOLVE TO:

SCENE 6: INTERNAL SEQUENCE. DAY. PEEBLESES' KIT-CHEN AND BEDROOM.

Edie's voice: The day after the plane landed Mrs. Peebles put both children in the car and drove them over to Chelsey, to get their hair cut. I loved being left in the house, alone. . . .

(Establish that Edie is alone in the house. SOUND of car leaving; she can wave through kitchen window, perhaps children's voices calling good-bye. She fusses around the kitchen a bit, then heads deliberately but with some air of caution or trepidation for the master bedroom.)

I had been in Mrs. Peebles' bedroom plenty of times, cleaning, and I always took a good look in her closet, at the clothes she had hanging there. . . . I wouldn't have looked in her bureau drawers, but a closet is open to anybody . . . That's a lie, I would have looked in the drawers, but I would have felt worse doing it and been more scared she could tell. . . .

(Edie looking into Mrs. Peebles' closet, considering, fingering, finally drawing out the satin evening-dress, admiring it, then very quickly chucking off her own outer clothes and putting it on. Looking in the mirror, pinning up her hair, helping herself to make-up, jewellery, more and more daring, showing a sense of her own elegance.)

All the excitement made me thirsty. The Peebleses drank ginger-ale or fruit drinks all day, like water, and I was getting so I did too. Also there was no limit on ice cubes, which I was so fond of I would even put them in a glass of milk. . . .

She walks with an air of consequence into the kitchen, opens the refrigerator, pours herself a glass of ginger-ale, gets out the ice cubes, etc. At some point during this we see Chris watching her through the screen door. When she has shut the refrigerator door and turns, glass in hand, she sees him too, and jumps, looks at once to see if she has spilled ginger-ale on the dress.

Chris: I never meant to scare you. I knocked but you were getting the ice out, you didn't hear me . . . *(No response from Edie.)* I'm from the plane over there. My name is Chris Watters, and I was wondering, could I use your pump?

Edie: You're welcome.

Chris: Were you going to a dance? Or is that the way the ladies around here generally get dressed up in the afternoon? *(Edie is overcome with embarrassment.)* You live here? Are you the lady of the house?

Edie: I'm the hired girl.

Chris: Well I just wanted to tell you, you look very nice. I got a surprise when I looked in the door and saw you, you looked so nice and beautiful. *(Edie would like to answer but is unable. Chris understands her embarrassment, smiles, and turns to go.)*

Edie: *(Calling after him)* We have piped water in the house. Save you pumping.

Chris: I don't mind the exercise. Thank you.

Edie: *(Faintly)* You're welcome. *(She goes to the window and watches him as long as there is a sound of pumping.)*

END OF ACT ONE

ACT TWO
SCENE 7: EXTERNAL SEQUENCE. NIGHT. FAIRGROUNDS WITH PLANE AND TENT.
Edie comes out of the house. The plane is in the fairgrounds with the tent beside it.

Chris sitting outside his tent, smoking, in the moonlight. Edie comes around the plane.

Chris: Hello. Were you looking for a plane ride? I don't start taking people up until tomorrow. . . . *(Recognizing her)* Oh, it's you. I didn't know you without your long dress on. *(After a long moment)* Did you want a ride? Sit down. Have a cigarette.

(Edie sits down, takes the cigarette, looks as if she wants to say something but can't. She is considerably alarmed.)

Put it in your mouth or I can't light it. It's a good thing I'm used to shy ladies. *(Lighting her cigarette)* Look at your hand shaking. Did you just want to have a chat, or what?

Edie: *(In a rush)* I wished you wouldn't say anything about that dress.

Chris: What dress? Oh-oh. That long dress.

Edie: It's hers. It's Mrs. Peebles's.

Chris: Whose? The lady you work for? Is that so? She wasn't home so you got dressed up in her dress, eh? You got dressed up and played queen. I don't blame you. You're not smoking that cigarette right. Don't just puff. Draw it in. Did nobody ever show you how to inhale? Are you scared I'll tell on you? Is that it? *(Edie, with difficulty, indicates yes.)* Well I won't. I won't in the slightest way mention it or embarrass you. Word of honour. *(Changing the subject in an effort to put her at her ease)* What do you think of my sign?

Propped against the tent-pole we see the sign, not very skilfully lettered.

> *See the World from the Sky*
> *Adults $1.00, Children 50¢*
> *Qualified Pilot*

Chris: My old sign was getting pretty beat-up. Thought I'd make up a new one. I'm not an expert at sign-making.

Edie: It's very good.

Chris: I don't need it for publicity. Word of mouth is usually enough. I turned away two carloads tonight. I just felt like taking it easy. I didn't tell them ladies were dropping in to visit me. *(Edie gets up.)* Do you have to go so soon?

Edie: They all went to the show. I have to get back. *(Starts away, then remembers her manners.)* Thank you for the cigarette.

Chris: Don't forget! You have my word of honour!

Edie runs back to the house. Chris sits, smoking, looking after her.

DISSOLVE TO:

SCENE 8: EXTERNAL SEQUENCE. DAY. PEEBLESES' YARD.

The mailman is pulling away in his car from the mailbox.

Chris pumping water in the Peebleses' yard. Edie on the porch, peeling vegetables, half-turned aside, half-hidden by an awning or lattice-work, pretending not to watch. When his pail is full he calls to her.

Chris: Hey! Why don't you come over? I'll take you up in my plane.

Edie: *(Slightly more confident now, smiles.)* I'm saving my money.

Chris: For what? For getting married? *(Edie laughs.)* I'll take you up for free if you come some time when it's slack. I really thought you'd come. I thought you'd like another cigarette.

Edie makes a face at him to be quiet. Mrs. Peebles comes out, freshly made-up, casual, slightly—cautiously—flirtatious. This is not lost on Edie.

Mrs. Peebles: How's business?

Chris: Not so bad.

Mrs. Peebles: Where did you learn to fly a plane?

Chris: In the war.

Mrs. Peebles: You like doing what you're doing?

Chris: I can't seem to settle down to anything else.

Mrs. Peebles: Sometimes I don't think I'm settled down myself. I wasn't brought up to live in the country. It's all my husband's idea. *(Chris smiles, waits, lets her extend herself, used to this kind of half-invitation.)* Maybe you ought to give flying lessons.

Chris: Would you take them?

They laugh. Edie has been listening to this exchange with a certain amount of gloom and jealousy, sensing undercurrents she can't really identify.

DISSOLVE TO:

SCENE 9: EXTERNAL SEQUENCE. DAY. PEEBLESES' YARD.

Sunday afternoon. The plane is taking off. Dr. and Mrs. Peebles, Edie, the two children, in the yard, watching the activity across the road. Some commotion, perhaps children cutting across the yard.

Alice Kelling's car turns into the drive, stops, Loretta Bird jumping out at once, Alice Kelling getting out more sedately, uncertainly.

Loretta: This here lady is looking for the man that flies the plane.

Alice Kelling: I'm sorry to bother you. I'm Alice Kelling, Mr. Watters' fiancée.

Loretta: I heard her asking in the coffee shop and I brought her out.

Dr. Peebles: He's up in the air right now but you're welcome to sit and wait. I'm Harry Peebles. My wife Glenna. He comes and gets his water here and he hasn't been over yet.

Alice Kelling: *(Straining to look at the sky)* That is him, then?

We see the plane swooping low, coming in for a landing.

Dr. Peebles: He's not in the habit of running out on you, is he, taking a different name? *(Laughter. Alice Kelling should appear nervously cordial, reserved and apologetic by turns, preoccupied.)* Couldn't we have some iced tea, Glenna?

Mrs. Peebles: Of course. Will you, Edie? *(To Alice)* Mr. Watters never mentioned that he had a fiancée.

Edie goes into the kitchen, where she gets out glasses, slices lemons, etc., preparing iced tea, doing this with her usual care, but all the time listening to the conversation coming from outside, occasionally peering out the window, an appraising look we know is directed at Alice Kelling. Having finished, she comes out with a tray and drinks.

Edie's voice: I loved fixing iced tea with lots of ice and slices of lemon in tall glasses. I ought to have mentioned before Dr. Peebles was an abstainer, at least around the house, or I wouldn't have been allowed to take the place. I had to fix a glass for Loretta Bird too, though it galled me, and when I went out she had settled in my lawn chair, leaving me the steps. . . .

Loretta: *(Somewhat proprietary)* Miss Kelling is a registered nurse. I knew as soon as I heard you in the coffee shop you was something like that. Was that how you met him, nursing?

Alice Kelling: Chris? Yes. Yes, it was.

Mrs. Peebles: *(Her cordiality too has slight reservations.)* Oh? Were you overseas?

Alice Kelling: No, it was before. When he was stationed at Centralia. He had a ruptured appendix. We got engaged and then he went overseas. *(When she talks of Chris in the past tense she is more secure.)*

Loretta: Youse've had a long engagement.

Edie offers the tray of glasses to Alice Kelling, who helps herself, sips, speaks composedly.

Alice Kelling: My, this is refreshing, after a long drive.

Dr. Peebles: He'll be glad to see you. It's a rackety kind of life, isn't it, never staying in one place long enough to really make friends.

Alice Kelling: I ought to phone the hotel. When I was offered directions I just came straight out.

Dr. Peebles: Why stay five miles away from him? Here you're right across the road. We've got rooms on rooms, look at this big house.

Mrs. Peebles: *(Just a bit late taking this up)* Yes. We have plenty of room. *(Catches sight of Chris coming across the road, calls gaily, challengingly)* Company for you!

Alice Kelling: Chris! *(Rising)* Here I am come chasing after you to see what you've been up to! *(She goes to meet him. Eyes of all the female spectators are on them as they kiss, formally.)*

Chris: You're going to spend a lot on gas that way.

Dr. Peebles: Stay for supper, Chris, won't you?

As Chris Watters turns with Alice's hand on his shoulder, Edie's eyes stray to the ring on her hand. It is a very small stone.

Mrs. Peebles: Yes, do. We'll eat outside. *(She goes into the house.)*

Loretta: Outside, with all them bugs?

Chris: Thanks. No more rides today, then. *(To Alice)* After supper we'll go into town.

Edie is watching, as Chris leads Alice to the table, pulling a chair out for her politely.

DISSOLVE TO:

SCENE 10: INTERNAL SEQUENCE. NIGHT. EDIE'S ROOM.
Edie lies in bed, wakeful, listening. When a car's lights sweep over the wall, she gets up, crouches by the window, watches.

CUT TO:

SCENE 11: EXTERNAL SEQUENCE. NIGHT. PEEBLESES' YARD.
Alice Kelling gets out of the driver's seat of her car, Chris out of the other side. She looks at him across the car as if she would be glad enough of an embrace, some further words, but won't risk asking for them; she must be careful with him.

He pretends not to notice. He mouths her a cheerful good-night, with a wave, or motion of his hand, that is kindly, mocking, apologetic, and implacable, all at once. He hurries into the dark and she, more slowly, enters the house.

Edie gets back into bed and lies on her back, thinking, stroking her arms.

FADE OUT.

END OF ACT TWO

ACT THREE
FADE IN:
SCENE 12: EXTERNAL SEQUENCE. DAY. PEEBLESES' YARD.
Alice Kelling, Mrs. Peebles, Joey, Heather, with towels, bathing-

suits, etc., getting into Alice Kelling's car. Edie handing in packages of sandwiches, fruit, thermos.

Alice Kelling: *(Looking at the sky)* I don't suppose he'll mind if I don't stay around watching him take off and come down all day.

Mrs. Peebles: You'll have a better time at the lake. He's not that fascinating to watch, is he?

Alice Kelling: I wish I could have told him.

Mrs. Peebles: Edie'll tell him. Don't worry.

Alice Kelling: *(Dubious look at Edie)* Five o'clock. Tell him we'll be no later than five o'clock.

They settle in the car and drive off.

DISSOLVE TO:

SCENE 13: INTERNAL SEQUENCE. DAY. KITCHEN.
Edie goes into the house, looks at the clock, turns on the oven, and begins, with precision and enthusiasm, to assemble the makings of a cake.

Edie's voice: I didn't see that he would be concerned about knowing this right away, and I thought of him eating whatever he ate over there, alone, cooking on his camp stove, so I got to work.

We see Edie at various phases of preparing, stirring, baking, and decorating, until the final product emerges at the end of the montage. We note that it is a cake. Edie wraps the pan in a towel and leaves the kitchen.

DISSOLVE TO:

SCENE 14: EXTERNAL SEQUENCE. DAY. FAIRGROUNDS WITH TENT AND PLANE.
Edie, crossing to the fairgrounds, sees the sign—a piece of paper tacked over the original sign: "No More Rides Today. Apologies." Carefully carrying the cake-pan wrapped in a dishtowel, she walks around the plane, pauses in front of the closed tent flap, knocks on the pole.

Edie's voice: *(While walking towards the tent)* . . . I didn't do anything to myself but take off my apron and comb my hair. I would like to have put some make-up on, but I was too afraid it would remind him of the way he first saw me, and that would humiliate me all over again. . . .

CUT TO:

SCENE 15: INTERNAL SEQUENCE. DAY. TENT.
Inside the tent. Chris lying on the cot, smoking.

Chris: *(Not enthusiastically)* Come in. *(Edie pushes up the flap.)* Oh, it's you. I'm sorry. *(Getting up)* I didn't know it was you.

Edie: I brought a cake and hope you're not sick.

Chris: Why would I be sick? Oh, that sign. No, I'm just tired of talking to people. I don't mean you. Have a seat. *(He gets up and fastens back the flap.)* Get some fresh air in here.

Edie: Your fiancée's gone to the lake. Her and Mrs. Peebles and Joey and Heather all went in her car. *(Chris grunts, trying to get a piece of the cake. Edie takes a knife concealed in the dish-towel and cuts it for him.)* She said be sure and tell you they'd be back by five o'clock.

Chris: Good. *(Apparently he means the cake. He eats a large piece rather quickly.)*

Edie: You could put the rest away for when you're hungry later.

Chris wraps the cake up.

Chris: I'll tell you a secret. I'm not going to be around here much longer.

Edie: Are you getting married?

Chris: Ha, ha. What time did you say they'd be back?

Edie: Five o'clock.

Chris: Well, by then this place'll have seen the last of me. A plane travels faster than a car. *(He absently unwraps and eats another piece of cake.)*

Edie: Now you'll be thirsty.

Chris: *(Nodding)* Water in the pail.

Edie: I could get you some fresh. I could bring some ice from the refrigerator.

Chris: No. I don't want you to go. I want a nice long time of saying good-bye to you.

Edie is not quite sure what a nice long good-bye means but decides that it is probably something pleasant and sits down on the cot.

Edie: Okay.

Chris: Are you going back to school in the fall?

Edie: Yes—no. I don't think so.

Chris: I guess you're just like me. I didn't much like school either.

Edie: I did okay. Except not really.

Chris: What do you like doing?

Edie: Well, you know. Cooking, cleaning, keeping house. I like doing that.

Chris moves closer to Edie and touches her hair.

Chris: Did you learn to bake at home?

Edie: Sure. Have a house without a pie, be ashamed until you die.

Chris: *(Laughing)* What's that?

Edie: *(Laughing as well)* I don't know. Just something my mother always says.

She does not pull away as Chris runs his finger along the side of her neck. He still has not sat down beside her on the cot, but stands next to her, thoughtfully exploring her face with his hand. She sits somewhat rigidly, with her hands folded in her lap.

Chris: *(Softly)* Tell me, has anyone ever done that to you?

Edie: *(Closing her eyes)* What?

Chris: Touch your face. Do you like it?

Edie: *(Passively delighted)* It's okay.

Chris sits beside her on the cot as Edie's narration begins. During the narration we pull back from Edie's face, as Chris begins kissing her, through the open flap of the tent until we see the tent and parts of the plane in the foreground.

Edie's voice: He sat beside me and started those little kisses, so soft, I can't ever let myself think about them. Such kindness in his face and lovely kisses, all over my eyelids and neck and ears, all over. Then me kissing back as well as I could (I had only kissed a boy on a dare before, and kissed my own arms for practice). And we lay back on the cot and pressed together, just gently. . . . It was lovely in the tent, that smell of grass and hot tent-cloth with the sun beating down on it. . . .

Chris comes out of the tent and splashes water from the pail on his face and neck, then goes back inside the tent and pours the rest of the water over Edie.

Chris: That's to cool us off, miss. *(He shakes himself dry in the sun, then comes back to Edie and takes her face in his hands.)* I'm going to write you a letter. I'll tell you where I am and maybe you can come and see me. Would you like that? Okay, then. You wait.

CUT TO:

SCENE 16: EXTERNAL SEQUENCE. DAY. FAIRGROUNDS.
Edie comes out of the tent and walks back towards the house.

  Chris stands in front of the tent and waves at her once, as she looks back.

FADE OUT.

END OF ACT THREE

ACT FOUR
SCENE 17: INTERNAL SEQUENCE. DAY. THE PEEBLESES'
KITCHEN.
Alice Kelling and Mrs. Peebles drinking coffee, Edie busy with something at the counter.

  Loretta Bird opens the screen door with the most perfunctory knock, sticks her head in.

Loretta: I see he's took off.

Alice Kelling: What? *(She pushes back her chair, hurries to the door.)* He's up with a passenger, isn't he?

Loretta: My kids come and told me this afternoon he was taking down his tent. Did he think he'd run through all the business there was around here? He never took off without letting you know, did he?

Alice Kelling sits down again, gets out her cigarettes, summons all her self-possession.

Alice Kelling: He'll send me word. He'll probably phone me tonight. He's so terribly restless, since the war.

Mrs. Peebles: Edie, he didn't mention anything to you, did he? When you took the message?

Edie: Yes.

Mrs. Peebles: Well, why didn't you say so? Did he say where he was going?

Edie: He said he might try Bayfield.

Edie is, of course, lying. She does this without hesitation, to save Chris from his fiancée's pursuit, and to keep him for herself, but she is a bit startled, once she has done it.

Alice Kelling: Bayfield. How far is that?

Mrs. Peebles: Thirty miles. Thirty-five.

Alice Kelling: Oh, well. That's not far. That's really not far at all. It's on the lake, isn't it? I could drive there tonight.

Edie's voice: You'd think I'd be ashamed of myself, setting her on the wrong track. . . . Women should stick together and not do things like that. I see that now but didn't then. I never thought of myself as being in any way like her, or coming to the same troubles, ever.

Alice's relief is clouded by suspicion as she looks at Edie.

Alice Kelling: When did he mention this to you?

Edie: Earlier.

Alice Kelling: When you were over at the plane?

Edie: Yes.

Alice Kelling: *(Smiling)* You must have stayed and had a chat. You must have had a little visit with him.

Edie: *(Feeling cornered)* I took a cake.

Mrs. Peebles: *(Rather sharply)* We didn't have a cake.

Edie: I baked one.

Alice Kelling: That was very friendly of you.

Loretta: Did you get permission? You never know what these girls'll do next. It's not they mean harm, so much as they're ignorant.

Mrs. Peebles: The cake is neither here nor there. Edie, I wasn't aware you knew Mr. Watters that well.

Alice Kelling: I'm not surprised. I suspected by the look of her as soon as I saw her. Little country tramps. We get them at the hospital all the time. Having their babies. We have to put them in a special ward because of their diseases. Fourteen and fifteen years old. You should see the babies they have, too. *(This speech should start out controlled, hard, hostile, and end in desperation, near hysteria.)*

Loretta: There was a bad woman here in town had a baby that pus was running out of its eyes.

Mrs. Peebles: Wait a minute. What is this talk? Edie. What about you and Mr. Watters? Were you intimate with him?

Edie: *(In a low voice but not without pride)* Yes.

Mrs. Peebles: Well. I am surprised. I think I need a cigarette. *(To Alice Kelling)* This is the first of any such tendencies I've seen in her.

Alice Kelling: *(Closer and closer to hysterical tears which finally break through)* Loose little bitch! Loose little bitch, aren't you? I knew as soon as I saw you. Men despise girls like you. He just made use of you and went off, you know that, don't you? Girls like you are just nothing, they're just public conveniences, just filthy little rags.

Mrs. Peebles: *(Trying to calm things down, disturbed by this explicitness)* Oh, now.

Alice Kelling: Filthy! Filthy little rag!

Loretta: *(She enjoys this scene enormously.)* Don't get yourself upset. Men are all the same.

Mrs. Peebles: Edie, I'm very surprised. I thought your parents were so strict. You don't want to have a baby, do you?

Edie: *(Suddenly seems much younger than she has up until now, begins to cry like an outraged child.)* You don't get a baby just from doing that!

Loretta: You see. Some of them are that ignorant.

Mrs. Peebles gets up and goes over to Edie and begins to shake her arms, firmly though not unkindly.

Mrs. Peebles: Calm down. Don't get hysterical. Calm down. Stop crying. Listen to me. Listen, I'm wondering if you know what being intimate means. Now tell me. What did you think we meant?

Edie: *(Still howling)* Kissing.

Mrs. Peebles: Oh, Edie. Stop it. Don't be so silly. It's all right. It's all a misunderstanding. Being intimate means a lot more than that. Oh, I *wondered.*

Alice Kelling: She's trying to cover up now. Yes. She's not so stupid. She sees she got herself in trouble.

Mrs. Peebles: I believe her. *(She puts her hands to her head.)* Oh. This is an awful business, all this.

Alice Kelling: Well. There is one way to find out. After all, I am a nurse.

Perhaps she could look at her hands or flex her fingers a bit during this speech. Perhaps nothing so obvious. But there should be a strong feeling of menace, bewildering Edie and exciting Loretta. Mrs. Peebles is at first amazed by the raw vengefulness, the vulgarity, of the idea—it is this she is aware of as much as the plight of Edie— then angered.

Mrs. Peebles: No. No. Go to your room, Edie. And stop that noise. *(She looks at Alice Kelling.)* That is too disgusting.

Edie runs out of the kitchen. The three women look after her.

DISSOLVE TO:

SCENE 18: INTERNAL SEQUENCE. DUSK. EDIE'S ROOM. She lies on the bed, still weeping, not desperately, but in reaction, trying to control each wave as it comes over her.

The sound of a car starting, driving away.

Mrs. Peebles appears in the doorway.

Mrs. Peebles: She's gone. Both of them are gone. Of course you know you should never have gone near that man and that is the cause of all this trouble. What do you know about a man like that? *(After a long moment)* I have a headache. As soon as you can, you go and wash your face in cold water and get at the dishes and we will not say any more about this.

During this speech Edie is gradually getting control of her sobs, the expression of her face grows calmer, even a bit dreamy and withdrawn; we should if possible be able to see her "putting this out of her mind", turning back to her memories and expectations.

DISSOLVE TO:

SCENE 19: EXTERNAL SEQUENCE. DAY. THE PEEBLESES' YARD.

Edie is waiting by the mailbox, happy, expectant. The mailman's car pulls up and she gives him a careless, confident smile, the overflow of her own pleasant secrets.

He hands her the mail.

Mailman: You got the smile I been waiting on all day! *(Edie glances quickly through the mail, is just faintly, briefly, disappointed, smiles again. Mailman, pulling away)* I'm getting so I'd miss it if I didn't see you here!

CUT TO:

SCENE 20: EXTERNAL SEQUENCE. DAY. VARIOUS ANGLES OF YARD, ROAD, MAILBOX.

Edie's voice: It never crossed my mind for the longest time that a letter might not come. I believed in it coming just like I believed the sun would rise in the morning. I just put off my hope from day to day.

SHOT *of Edie (perhaps a* LONG SHOT*) waiting, greeting the mailman, looking through the mail, as before.*

SHOT *of Edie wearing a sweater, goldenrod around the mailbox (unmistakably a fall scene), taking one envelope, obviously not the right one, from the mailman, remembering to smile at him, walking away.*

Till it just struck me: *No letter was ever going to come.*

Maybe a SHOT *of the mailbox here, and /or the empty, darkening fairgrounds, where the plane had been.*

I thought of women doing this all their lives. Waiting and waiting by the mailbox for one letter or another. I was never made to go on like that. If there's two kinds of women, one kind waiting and the other kind busy and not waiting, I knew which kind I had to be.

The mailman drives up to the mailbox where Edie is waiting again. This time, however, instead of holding the mail out to her, he stops the car and half opens the door.

Mailman: Got nothing for you today.

Edie: Nothing?

Mailman: Not even a Hydro bill. . . . Hey, there's a good movie in Goderich on Saturday. Would you like to come?

Edie looks at the mailman, surprise turning to pleasure in her eyes. She nods.

Edie: Okay.

Mailman: Okay then. I'll pick you up at six. (*He closes the door of his car and drives away. Edie looks after him.*)

Edie's voice: I went out with the mailman for two years and we were engaged a year more before we got married. He always tells the children how I went after him, sitting by the mailbox day after day, and naturally I don't let on any different. Why shouldn't people think what pleases them and makes them happy?

FADE OUT.

ROLL CLOSING TITLES OVER SHOT *of mailman driving his car, whistling happily.*

Friends and Relations

Hugh Hood

Sam Tata, Montreal

Friends and Relations

Hugh Hood

NOTE: The short story "Friends and Relations" appeared in 1973 in the literary journal *Seven Persons Repository*. The television play which follows is a completely new and free treatment of the same material in dramatic form, written especially for the CBC television series *The Play's the Thing*.

Millicent Holman wept incoherently, self-indulgently, and without real sorrow, sitting in the bathtub splashing water on her pretty face and, as always, refusing to think through a matter which genuinely puzzled her. She left such exercises to her husband. Faced with a puzzle or a mystery, especially if other people were involved, she preferred simply to stare at it with her pretty pout, hoping that it would solve itself or disappear.

"I'm hopeless, I know," she wailed without meaning it. She was by no means hopeless; she was very young-looking, had a little money inherited from a great-aunt, and had stayed married, and in fact meant to go on staying married.

"I can't understand mother at all," she moaned, her voice muffled by bubbles. She fished around for the soap, seized it, and began to scrub her back and shoulders energetically.

"Do me lower down!" she commanded her husband, who was shaving.

James Holman put down his razor with an imperceptible sigh, twisted his face into a grimace at the mirror, and bending began to soap his wife's back. He felt the soap bump over her vertebrae with a seesaw motion.

"There's no need to cry," he said hopefully, "she'll come another time." He admired his mother-in-law, the redoubtable Mrs. Lawson Bird, genuinely and extravagantly, and never quite knew what she was up to.

"I'm her only daughter," wept Millicent, "and I love her dearly. And she refuses to come and see us."

"She doesn't refuse to see us," said James calmly, "she'll come and see us, all right. She simply has other things to think about."

"She shouldn't have other things to think about," said Millicent pettishly, quite aware of her tone and position, "she hasn't been to see us in over a year. She hasn't seen the baby walk or talk." She rinsed herself and stood up, a column of pearly pink marble, a Venus of the bathtub. Botticellian.

Her husband regarded her admiringly, in spite of himself. "She must have three hundred pictures of Jassy," he said, turning to finish his interrupted shave. Millicent tossed her head, threw on her house-coat, and sidled past him into their bedroom. He was obliged to wipe the steam off the shaving mirror a second time. Millicent habitually filled the tub to the brim with steaming hot water.

"Pictures aren't the same," he heard her complain from the bed-room, "and I wonder what she's doing in Montreal."

He began to laugh cheerfully; he was looking forward to their evening out. "I'm sure I know," he said lewdly.

Millicent was as usual scandalized by the hint.

When Millicent Holman's father, Doctor Lawson Bird, had died three years before, he had been the best known dentist in eastern Ontario, and among the best technically. He had not been trained as a specialist but had acquired a very considerable proficiency in oral surgery over the years, and had cases referred to him from a hundred miles away. But much more than his professional attainments, which were quite real and valuable, his hobbies and activities had made him widely known.

He had, for example, played semi-pro hockey every winter until he was past forty and it was widely rumored that as a younger man he had turned down professional offers and might have played for the Maple Leafs if his career hadn't intervened. This was not strictly true. He had never been a fast enough skater to be a professional but he played excellent Senior-B hockey with locally sponsored teams. He was a stocky rough defenseman, known on the sports pages of many small eastern Ontario weeklies as "the denting dentist" or "the extract" in reference to his habit of scoring crucial last-period goals.

He had founded the Stoverville Camera Club and was an excellent amateur photographer who had sold news and candid shots to the Toronto papers. He owned two boats, a launch for trolling and a one-design sloop which he raced, and in the summer was on the Saint Lawrence at every moment that could be spared from his extensive practice. He belonged to an exclusive hunting lodge owned by several rich friends of his in Stoverville, which is a town with money in it. He played a fair game of golf, collected records—his taste running as high as Brahms—and was in short a man of solid professional worth and many graceful and attractive personal accomplishments. When he was alive, the people who came to the Birds' home were either his friends or relatives—he belonged to an enormous and enormously ramified old family—or his former classmates at Stoverville Collegiate Institute.

Mrs. Bird seemed to prefer to stay in the background. Her husband was so popular, so widely known, so genuinely loved and admired, and her daughter—their only child—such a vivid, gay girl, that the Birds' friends and relations hardly remembered that Mrs. Bird was around the house at all, except, of course, at mealtime.

She had been trained as a nurse before her marriage and spent long hours nursing the dozen elderly invalids who composed the senior stratum of Doctor Bird's family connection, suffering many disappointments and rebuffs in this charitable and kindly activity. These old people were hard—immensely hard—to please. Some of them were absolute monsters of senile rancor; she was accused regularly of theft, sometimes of intrigue, and it was made plain to her that she was only a Bird by marriage.

One ancient aunt of Doctor Bird's, after Mrs. Bird had spent ten years in caring for her during her decline, actually, specifically and by name, cut her out of her will, charging that she was an unworthy wife for Doctor Lawson.

Mrs. Bird said nothing to this; she knew what the old and sick can imagine as they lie in bed with nothing to do but stoke the fires of their resentment. She knew that she had been kindness itself to the old aunt.

She didn't let herself be daunted; everyone in the family must know that what Aunt Sarah asserted was false, or if they didn't they certainly should have. The one great reward that Mrs. Bird looked for was the opportunity to take care of Lawson, really at last to be able to do something for him, if his health should fail before hers.

But she was denied the chance. Three years ago Doctor Bird suffered a coronary attack while trolling on the river. By the time his companion could get him ashore he was beyond help. He died during the night in the Stoverville General, quite literally mourned by everyone who had known him.

He had served as Chairman of the Board of Education for several years and the Stoverville schools were closed on the day following his death and on the following Monday, the day of the funeral.

He was only fifty-four years old and had just begun to earn more than he spent, which was a lot. He had always lived on a large scale, had been a free and generous spender, and the cost of his multitudinous hobbies and interests had been very great. He had for example just bought an enormous outboard motor, paid cash for it, and never used it. When it finally came to be sold, it brought Mrs. Bird about one-fifth what the Doctor had paid for it. It was, by this time, a last year's model, and it was hard to find a buyer.

It became evident very speedily that Ruthie, as Mrs. Bird was known in the family, was going to be left with very little. When the final balance came to be set, what was left was a few thousand in cash and the value of the outstanding accounts at the office. Mrs. Bird felt no surprise or disappointment on the score of her inheritance. She had known vaguely that her husband's insurance program was not in satisfactory shape. He had alluded to it once or twice in passing, saying that he had bought his insurance in the late thirties, and that while it had seemed like enough at the time, it certainly wasn't these days. He had been meaning to do something about it but had gone along putting it off.

It was a stroke of good fortune that Millicent's wedding had taken place a few months before the Doctor's death instead of afterwards. It had cost him thousands, money which came from current income and from the sale of a piece of riverfront property he had been hanging on to for years; he had intended to build a combination boathouse, cottage, and hunting lodge on it. But he gladly spent the money on the wedding instead. After the ceremony James and Millicent had moved to the United States to live and they were not in Stoverville when the Doctor died.

When they heard, in the middle of the night, they were surprised and shocked. In the morning they started up from Connecticut by car, arriving in time to attend the beginnings of the solemn family council which began the evening after Doctor Lawson died and continued at intervals for over a year. All were perplexed at "poor Ruthie's" situation, and they grew more perplexed and reluctant to make any positive cash commitments as the facts concerning the Doctor's estate grew clearer.

"Of course you can come and live with me, Ruthie," said old Aunt Cleila, her eyes moist and glittering, "Lawson would want you to."

"No, I don't believe I will," said Mrs. Bird positively, with an unfamiliar briskness. The old aunts and uncles were a trifle taken aback at her brusquerie. They had been so used to her habitual self-effacement that it came as a surprise to them to see her make a choice of her own.

She told her son-in-law much later that Aunt Cleila had discharged her housemaid as soon as she heard about Lawson, meaning to have "poor Ruthie" supply the gap.

"What do they think I am?" she asked James, strictly privately. "Do they imagine that I don't know what a housemaid gets paid these days?"

James grinned. "I won't invite you to Hartford," he said. "I don't want you thinking such things about us."

"Gracious," she said, with the faintest touch of asperity, "I know I can come to you at any time, James." She smiled at him kindly, almost, he suspected, patronizingly. "You must lead a pretty quiet life these days," she hazarded.

"We do," he assented, wondering what she was really thinking.

The aunts and uncles, and Doctor Bird's cousins and connections, who between them dominated Stoverville society—for there is "society" even in Stoverville—were aghast at Ruthie's cavalier dismissal of Aunt Cleila's offer. They decided amongst themselves that she must be holding out for something more comfortable. She had, they estimated, enough money to live on for about two years. When that was exhausted her independence would be much reduced. They could hardly contain themselves for so long.

"Come to us and care for the children. We'll pay you a small honorarium and you'll have your nights free," said Cousin Roger, the Cadillac dealer.

"Oh, Roger, don't you see," she smiled inflexibly, "it's been fifteen years since I had anything to do with young children." Cousin Roger, who knew a thing or two about the management of staff, domestic and business, felt that he had met his match.

Finally Uncle Maurice came to see her one night, in all the weight of his seniority as the oldest male member of the family. He had always liked Ruthie, and found her pale and uninteresting, though a good nurse. He was at this time Mayor of Stoverville.

"Now, look here, Ruthie," he told her kindly, "you won't be able to stay in this house much longer. After all, it doesn't belong to you."

It was true. It belonged to some Toronto cousins who meant to spend their retirement in Stoverville; they had let Doctor Lawson have it for a nominal rent while he lived. Now their retirement was approaching and they wanted the house.

"Grover and Pauline will be moving down here this summer," said the Mayor. "You don't want to be in their way when they come."

"Of course not, Uncle Maurice," said Ruthie with alacrity. The old man felt encouraged, and went on.

"I'm prepared to find you a good job downtown," he said. "I heard today that there's an opening for a saleslady in the Mode Shoppe."

"I don't think I'd like waiting on the people in Stoverville," said Mrs. Bird with a faint smile.

It was on the tip of Uncle Maurice's tongue to tell her that she had no choice; but something in her manner warned him and he held his peace.

"Won't you tell me," he said at length, in great puzzlement, "what you think you'd like to do?"

"Of course," she said pleasantly and with a funny composure. "I'd like to find something that will get me out of Stoverville for a while."

"Do you fancy anything in particular?" asked Uncle Maurice dryly. He had a glimmer of what was going through her head.

"Why, yes," she said, "I believe I'll have a try at real estate."

"Real estate?"

"Yes."

"I see," he said in amazement, "well . . . if I can help you in any way, Ruthie, I hope you'll let me know." He was really a nice old fellow, was Uncle Maurice.

"Perhaps you can swing some business my way," said Mrs. Bird cheerfully, as she showed him to the door.

Without waiting for the news of her decision to spread around town, Mrs. Bird placed the Accounts Receivable from the dental practice in the hands of a collection agency (an act which infuriated a great many of the late Doctor's clients), took what cash she had with her, and left for Toronto without saying good-bye to anyone. She caught on as a trainee with a big-time real estate broker, and for nine months made no sales, although she trailed hundreds of clients through development houses in the far-ranging Toronto suburbs.

She wrote to James and Millicent now and then, recounting her hilarious adventures and misadventures. A fifty-year-old Hungarian with extensive rooming-house properties was pursuing her (she was herself a year or two under fifty), escorting her to the Csardas Café for the two-dollar goulash dinner. He proposed marriage and the investment of her Accounts Receivable in more rooming houses for more immigrants. He also had a project for a Hungarian daily which he hoped she might back.

The manager of the branch office was swiping her clients as soon as she got them interested in anything, and closing with them.

"I don't mind that," she wrote, "because he knows I can turn him in to the Real Estate Board any time, so he gives me extra training. I didn't expect to make any money while I'm learning the tricks; it's like an apprenticeship. Anyway, it shows that I can soften a prospect up for the kill pretty well."

When James Holman read this, he laughed immoderately, in a way that made his wife very angry.

"I don't know what you're laughing at," Millicent said in the tones of extreme vexation; "that horrible man's simply taking advantage of her."

"Sure he is," said James, laughing, "and she knows it. She's terribly sharp. She knows they wouldn't dream of paying her while she's learning the business. This is all just experience. You wait!" and he paused to savor the prospect. "She'll go back to Stoverville and lay it waste."

Mrs. Bird passed the examinations which qualified her as a realtor with inordinately high marks. Then, her certificate in her bag and her training indelibly stamped in her mind, she descended on the Stoverville real estate market like a shrike upon doves. She took a bachelor apartment on the east side of town, got herself accepted as a saleswoman by the newest and most alert broker in town, and began to prowl all over town in her car, late into the evenings, making notes on the houses and affairs of all the people she knew, and on the prospects of their households breaking up. She knew the town and its inhabitants so well that she was better qualified than any of the other salesmen in the office.

None of the other people were Stoverville natives; they had all been shipped in from the home office in Toronto. None had so close a grasp of the local context, not even the branch-manager, who came to cherish her mightily. She knew which middle-aged couple was only waiting eagerly to marry off the last plain daughter before fleeing to Florida, what pair of rich youngsters had gone through three houses already and were seeking a fourth that might conform more closely to their notion of a love nest. She could gauge precisely the size of the fading old family fortunes which held the valuable riverfront properties along King Street, East, and understood before they did themselves which dowagers would soon be obliged to sell their huge houses in order to shut off the tax drain.

She anticipated all marriages, divorces, births, and deaths, and knew more vital statistics than the County Registrar. Soon she was making more sales than anyone in the office, even the manager; she was the first lady realtor that Stoverville had ever seen, a kind of albatross or Moby Dick, a "lusus naturae", a mysterious natural phenomenon.

Aunt Cleila deplored the turn of affairs because, although she herself was very comfortably fixed, holding much acreage out in the back concessions as well as her King Street house, her income was fixed and rather small. She guessed that "poor Ruthie" with only her tiny bachelor apartment to maintain would soon have more loose money to dispose of than she herself. She made a series of querulous phone calls around the family circle but obtained small sympathy.

Cousin Roger was wiser. He did his level best to sell Mrs. Bird a Cadillac, telling her that her new position virtually dictated the purchase.

"You can take six people out to see a house at once," he said, "and think of the impression you'll create."

She stared at him thoughtfully. "What do you think of these Volkswagen station wagons?"

Cousin Roger retired in chagrin.

Of them all, Uncle Maurice pursued the wisest course. He made no overture to Mrs. Bird, figuring that when she wanted to come and see him she would without being asked. Soon she was in and out of his office frequently, conferring with him on the financial backgrounds of her clients. Between them, she and Uncle Maurice knew enough about Stoverville equities to jail half the town.

In Hartford, Conn., Millicent and James were left to themselves almost completely. Mrs. Bird came to see them very briefly when Jassy was born and then hastened back to Stoverville pleading the excuse of a pending big deal. They asked her back repeatedly but her replies were evasive until finally they saw that it was useless and stopped asking her.

Just before she climbed into the bathtub, Millicent had been reading her mother's latest evasive note. She and James had had to hire a sitter in order to enjoy one of their rare evenings out. She thought irritatedly of other people's mothers and the quantity of free baby-sitting they afforded. In her letter, Mrs. Bird mentioned that she would be spending the next two weeks in Montreal, first at a realtors' convention, then in investigating the finances of a suspicious subdivider.

She was paying for the trip with the proceeds of her next-to-last big sale. She had succeeded in moving a famous old Stoverville white-elephant, a forty-room riverfront mansion that had been unoccupied for ten years and was impoverishing the owners with upkeep and tax charges. She had sold it to an order of teaching sisters as the nucleus of a convent boarding school. Her commission had been thirteen hundred. She was taking the manager of her office to dinner that night in Montreal; they had important matters to discuss.

Millicent began to shed tears, not of sorrow but of sheer annoyance. "I'm hopeless, I know," she wailed in extreme irritation, "but I can't understand mother at all."

James thought to himself that he had no complaints; they would certainly be Mrs. Bird's heirs, which, though a small, mean, and distant consolation for the denial of Mrs. Bird's company, was nevertheless a consolation. Unless, that is, he pondered, unless . . . he was not certain of her age but thought it sufficient.

"We'll be seeing her," he said, content to wait, "sooner or later. She's not interested in us. Why should she be? She has other fish to fry," and he thought of the two realtors conferring over dinner at Café Martin.

"Well, I think it's unnatural," complained Millicent.

"It's the most natural thing in the world," said James. He repeated it with satisfaction. "The most natural thing in the world."

He began to laugh to himself in a way which, he knew, always antagonized his wife.

Characters

MRS. SOLOMONS

CHRISTINE FLETCHER

JIM FLETCHER

MRS. CLAUDE HARKNESS

COUSIN STANLEY

UNCLE LOU

MRS. BIRD

SAMPSON WILLEY

LARRY GODFREY

ANDRAS SZEKELY

ACT ONE

FADE IN:

SCENE 1: EXTERNAL SEQUENCE. DAY. A RURAL CEME-TERY OUTSIDE STOVERVILLE.

MEDIUM SHOT. *We are looking at a recent grave, banked with flowers, still perhaps rimmed by the artificial turf sometimes used by undertakers. Around and behind the grave are weeds and tall grass. There is no* SOUND *on the track but that of the breeze.* Not *wind. A faint breeze. We see weeds and grass move with the light motion of the air. We move in to a* CLOSE SHOT *of the fresh flowers and the new headstone with its freshly chiselled inscription:*

Lawson Bird, M.D. Born 1920. Died 1974. *The* SOUND *of the breeze drops and there is a brief silence. Then, while we are still holding on the headstone we begin to hear the sound of conversation, not too animated, at the post-funeral reception in the Bird house in Stoverville. The sound of conversation rises quickly and we can hear clinking glasses and then we can distinguish voices for the opening two lines of dialogue.*

Mrs. Solomons: Are you going right back to Montreal, Christine?

Christine: Jim's leaving on Monday but I'm staying for a while, till Mother gets settled.

CUT TO:

SCENE 2: INTERNAL SEQUENCE. A DARK DAY. THE BIRD HOUSE IN STOVERVILLE.
The after-funeral reception in the Bird home. We are in the dining room by the door to the hall. The living room, hall, and dining room, where a buffet lunch is displayed, should all be visible. Strong late-Victorian, eastern-Ontario, small-city atmosphere. Mrs. Solomons is speaking to Christine Fletcher. We can see Jim Fletcher standing beside them.

Mrs. Solomons: Oh God, Chris, it's a shock . . . to lose somebody you've lived with for thirty years.

Christine: She's going to have a very difficult adjustment.

Mrs. Solomons shows signs of getting ready to leave. Business with hat and gloves, etc. She moves into the hall.

Mrs. Solomons: Sam is in obstetrics in Montreal . . . I guess you know.

Christine: I've been intending to phone him.

Mrs. Solomons: I wish you would. You and Jim are the only Stoverville people he knows in Montreal.

Christine: I'd love to see Sam. He's kind of like an old boy friend . . . but . . . you aren't leaving?

Mrs. Solomons: I think I will. It's a big turnout and the noise might tire Ruthie.

Christine: Everybody's been so thoughtful. I mean . . . look at all the food . . . those pies. *(She gestures widely at the range of dishes on the buffet. We should see various guests helping themselves.)*

Mrs. Solomons: There wasn't a better-known or better-liked man in

Stoverville than your father. I guess you know that. I'll say good-bye now, Christine.

Mrs. Solomons is seen exiting as Christine calls after her.

Christine: Oh goodbye, goodbye, and thanks for everything.

Jim Fletcher moves into the frame and continues the talk.

Jim: Isn't she nice? We'll have to be sure to phone Sam. Old boy friend or not.

Jim and Christine chuckle soberly together as Mrs. Claude Harkness appears. She is slightly tipsy and feeling it.

Mrs. Harkness: My dears, I simply had to come . . .

Jim: It's very kind . . .

Mrs. Harkness: *(Not about to be interrupted)* . . . to go off just like that. Makes you think, doesn't it? A coronary, they said. That was it, wasn't it, Chrissie?

Christine: I'm afraid so.

Mrs. Harkness: I just want to say, if there's anything Claude can do, now, any little thing. Just refer the patients to Claude.

Christine: Thank you.

Mrs. Harkness: *(Sidling off to the buffet for a refill on her glass of sherry)* He looked so natural, like he was asleep *(Voice fades)*.

Jim: Who was that?

Christine: Wasn't it Doctor Harkness's wife? She's aged since I saw her. I imagine things like this are kind of a diversion for her.

Jim and Christine remain talking together as the CAMERA PANS *slowly across to where Cousin Stanley and Uncle Lou are chatting in the dining room.*

Cousin Stanley: . . . well I literally begged him, Uncle Lou. I said, "Lawson, why don't you pay cash for this car? You can afford it."

Uncle Lou: Surely he had the payments insured.

Cousin Stanley: No thanks to him. It was me that put it in the contract. Lawson always thought he'd live forever.

Uncle Lou: He had a good life, Stan. He never had a care in the world. Hell, he was playing Senior "B" hockey when he was past forty.

Cousin Stanley: Yeah, and he had a heart attack that killed him before he was fifty-five.

Jim Fletcher comes over to join them.

Uncle Lou: Hello, Jim. We were talking about your mother-in-law's prospects. She isn't going to be any too well off, do you realize that?

Jim: Of course, if she absolutely *had* to she could always come and live with us in Montreal.

Cousin Stanley: She'll need a lot of help, Mr. Fletcher. Somebody to lean on.

Uncle Lou: Yes, it's a shame. The Doctor was a great man in his way. He'll be missed. I don't quite know how poor Ruth will survive.

Cousin Stanley: You know, Mr. Fletcher . . . Jim . . . she doesn't know what a safety-deposit box *is?* Nobody ever saw her. What with the Doctor so popular and Christine so pretty, you hardly realized poor Ruthie was in the house.

Jim: She's upstairs, resting.

CUT TO:

SCENE 3: INTERNAL SEQUENCE. THE SAME DARK AF-TERNOON ROOMS.
Looking up the staircase to the landing where Mrs. Bird stands with a photograph in her hand. The guests catch sight of her. Crowd noises.

Cousin Stanley: Here she is now, everybody.

Mrs. Harkness: She hasn't been crying anyway. She's been brave through it all.

Uncle Lou: Brave, yes. And pretty quiet.

Mrs. Bird: I was looking for this. Heavens, what a pile of junk in that attic.

STILL *of Doctor Bird in his old hockey uniform, with his widow's* VOICE OVER. *She addresses Christine.*

Mrs. Bird: Chris, darling, first thing Monday we'll have to get into the attic and throw things out. And some of the junk we can sell. Lawson's snowshoes. He bought them the winter we were married. Never used them that I can remember. *(Looks at photo.)* This is how I think of him, full of get up and go. *(Mrs. Bird begins to move downstairs.)*

Uncle Lou: He could have been a pro, Ruthie.

Mrs. Bird: No, I don't believe so, Uncle Lou. He wasn't a good enough skater and he'd never have left Stoverville. But me . . . I've never really given up the notion of being a city girl. *(As she says this she moves briskly down the last of the stairs and crosses the dining room towards a big window. People swirl around her and make way for her.)*

Christine: Mother, you can just pack up and come to Montreal.

Mrs. Bird: But Christine, your apartment's so poky, and in a while there'll be children . . .

Jim: You're very welcome, Mrs. Bird, any time at all.

Mrs. Bird: Maybe for weekends.

Cousin Stanley: You might do some baby-sitting for us, Ruthie. You adore the children.

Mrs. Bird: At a safe distance, Stanley. I haven't dealt with young children for twenty years.

Cousin Stanley: You'll have to work out something, Ruth. Lawson didn't leave much.

Mrs. Bird: *(To Uncle Lou)* I suppose that's right, isn't it, Uncle Lou, or should I say "Your Worship"?

Uncle Lou: Oh, goodness, Ruth. It just happens to be my turn to be Mayor . . . look here, how would it be if I came along over to see you? What about tomorrow morning? I handled Lawson's insurance, you know, and some other matters.

Mrs. Bird: I wish you would. Come along any time, please. I'll be here. *(She turns and addresses the crowd generally.)* And now won't you all have something to eat, and perhaps a drink? Lawson would want you to enjoy yourselves. *(To Cousin Stanley)* What about you, Stanley? You'd be more comfortable with something to drink. *(She goes to the dining-room buffet table and begins to pour drinks.)*

CUT TO:

SCENE 4: INTERNAL SEQUENCE. DAY. THE LIVING ROOM IN THE SAME SET.
The next morning. Much more sunshine showing. We see Mrs. Bird at a small writing-desk, adding up figures. We hear footsteps on the porch and the doorbell rings.

Mrs. Bird: *(To an off-camera hearer)* I'll get it. I'll get it. *(She gets* *up and goes to the front door, where she greets Uncle Lou.)* Good morning, Uncle Lou. Are you on your way to the office?

Uncle Lou: No, Ruthie, I want to take the whole morning to go over things with you.

Mrs. Bird: I wouldn't want you to lose a prospect.

Uncle Lou: They can look after prospects while I'm out of the office . . . at least I hope they can. And I want to take time to help you, Ruth. In a way I feel responsible. I feel that I allowed Lawson to neglect his affairs.

Mrs. Bird: He was half asleep most of the time. He made house calls at all hours, day or night. He had the right to spend his money as he pleased, and I'm glad he did because he enjoyed his life. I'm not apologizing for Lawson in any way.

Uncle Lou: Of course not, Ruth. But I should have kept after him all the same. I had policies waiting for his signature that he just never got around to. This house isn't yours, you know, and you couldn't afford to run it anyway. Eventually you'll have to go into an apartment.

Mrs. Bird: How much does it all add up to?

Uncle Lou: Let's see now, the car is free and clear . . . and you'll be getting eighteen thousand in insurance money, from policies Lawson bought around nineteen-fifty. About two thousand in a couple of bank accounts . . . comes to around twenty thousand, plus the car. The other big item is the accounts receivable at the office. Plenty of people owe you money. Lawson doesn't seem to have been very good about sending out bills.

Mrs. Bird: As long as there was enough coming in for us to get along, he didn't care about bills.

Uncle Lou: He was a funny guy. . . .

TIGHT CU *of Mrs. Bird's face. She speaks reflectively.*

Mrs. Bird: Yes . . . a funny guy.

This is Lawson's epitaph, in a way. They are silent for a moment.

Uncle Lou: Anyway, there's around ten thousand owing. You might get half of it.

Mrs. Bird: Is that all?

Uncle Lou: Hardest thing in the world, to collect a dead doctor's bills. Hardest thing in the world . . . there isn't the same sense of obligation.

Mrs. Bird: Five thousand maybe?

Uncle Lou: With luck. *And* it'll take six months and more to get them all in, *and* you'll have to go to a collection agency for some of them. That would give you around twenty-five thousand to invest and you could get a safe eight, eight and a quarter, say two thousand a year.

Mrs. Bird: I'll have to work.

Uncle Lou: The way prices are going you need to earn another three to four thousand a year just to keep yourself.

Mrs. Bird: I'm fifty. I'll have lots of time to work. *(She doesn't seem too displeased about this either.)*

Uncle Lou: I've taken the liberty of making a few enquiries. I think they'd pay you eighty a week at the Emmeline Shoppe. You must know a lot about ladies' wear.

Mrs. Bird: I wouldn't like waiting on my friends.

Uncle Lou: Have you got any ideas yourself?

Mrs. Bird: I believe I'll try real estate. I think I could sell homes— especially to women.

Uncle Lou: You wouldn't need much capital and you already own a car. I think that's a very good idea.

Mrs. Bird: Yes, I've thought of all that. *(She shows Uncle Lou to the door. She has a very pleased look. They both laugh in a friendly way through the last two lines.)*

Uncle Lou: As I say, if there's anything I can do to help . . . any good advice.

Mrs. Bird: Why, Your Worship, I'll be coming in all the time, to pick your brains.

CUT TO:

SCENE 5: INTERNAL SEQUENCE. NIGHT. THE BIRD HOUSE.
Same living room or small library as in previous scene. Christine and Jim in a very private consultation.

Jim: I don't want to be a fink, Chris, but I really don't see how we could fit her in permanently.

Christine: The thing is, we made her an offer.

Jim: It would be awfully squeezed if . . . I mean if . . .

Christine: *(Briskly. Less coy than Jim)* If I'm pregnant.

Jim: That's it. Would she have enough to get by on, do you think?

Christine: I doubt it. Apparently Dad spent everything as it came in. He probably thought he was good for another thirty years.

Jim: Do you think we're going to have to take care of her?

Christine: I think she'd sooner starve, if you really want to know. You can go back to Montreal with a clear conscience.

Jim: I have to go back. You know that.

Christine: I've got a funny feeling about Mother. I don't know why.
                                                            CUT TO:

SCENE 6: INTERNAL SEQUENCE. NIGHT. LIVING ROOM IN BIRD HOUSE.

Mrs. Bird: . . . and I asked you to come, Sampson, because you and Lawson were so close, and you were in the boat with him when it happened.

Sampson Willey: If we could have got him to shore faster, he might have been all right.

Mrs. Bird: I don't think so. It was a massive attack.

Sampson Willey: I can't help feeling responsible, all the same.

Mrs. Bird: Then perhaps you'll help me, I want to come into your office as a trainee, Sampson. I want to learn the real-estate business from scratch.

Willey: There's never been a woman realtor in Stoverville that I know of.

Mrs. Bird: I'll be the first. And you won't have to install a desk for me or anything. And I'll buy my own filing equipment and keep it in my apartment, when I find one.

Willey: The office isn't *that small.* We could fit in a filing cabinet.

Mrs. Bird: I figure with good luck I can qualify for a salesman's certificate over the winter.

Willey: There's an awful lot to learn . . . evaluation . . . the local tax situation.

Mrs. Bird: How to prepare an offer. Legal connections.

Willey: All that. How to manage a closing. And all the practical things like how to brush off somebody who's just looking.

Mrs. Bird: All those practical things. That's what I need to know.

Willey: *(Eyeing her speculatively)* You're sure you're not thinking of going out and opening your own office later on?

Mrs. Bird: Nothing at all like that. I just want to sell houses to women. I think I'd understand what a woman wants in a property. Cupboards. Closets. Storage space. The wife has a big say in the choice of a house, right?

Willey: Too big a say, in my opinion.

Mrs. Bird: Besides, I'm kind of an expert on Stoverville. I've had nearly thirty years to watch who's getting married or separated. Who died. Who might be thinking of selling their house, or buying one. Give me a try, Sampson. It won't cost you a thing.

Willey: I don't see why I shouldn't; you might bring in some new prospects. Tell you what, come along into the office on Monday, and we'll give it a try.

FADE OUT.

END OF ACT ONE

ACT TWO
FADE IN:
SCENE 7: EXTERNAL SEQUENCE. DAY. FRONT DOOR OF BIRD HOME.
About five months has elapsed and it is now early spring. We are at the doorway to the big veranda of the Bird house in bright sunshine. Christine, now obviously about five months pregnant, is at the door, talking to Cousin Stanley.

Christine: I know she's here some place, Stanley. She just popped in from the office. Come on in and sit down.

She leads him into the living room. He sits down and Christine goes off in search of her mother. Some changes in the set decor may be made here, to clear away junk and make the room look less cluttered. Mrs. Bird has spoken of moving into an apartment, but now almost half a year has gone by and she is still hanging on in her big old house. The point is not underlined in the dialogue, but the decor might make it quite subtly and agreeably. Cousin Stanley fans himself moodily with a piece of paper he holds in his hand.

Cousin Stanley: Bloody nerve she's got. And only a Bird by marriage at that. Never in thirty years. Not till this minute. Never!
Mrs. Bird enters very briskly.

Mrs. Bird: Good morning, Stanley, and what can I do for you? Can I sell you a house?

Cousin Stanley: I'm quite pleased with the house I've got, thank you all the same. I've been living in it since long before *you* ever came here.

Mrs. Bird: It's still heavily mortgaged, isn't it?

Cousin Stanley: How do you know?

Mrs. Bird: It's my business to know.

Cousin Stanley: You know more than you need to know. You never should have got mixed up with Sampson Willey. He's got more twists than a corkscrew. Did he put you up to this? *(He flourishes his piece of paper angrily.)*

Mrs. Bird: This what?

Cousin Stanley: In thirty years I never had a bill from Lawson, and now this. Nine hundred and fifty-seven dollars. I'm disappointed.

Mrs. Bird: Let's be accurate, Stanley. You've been billed every three months for years, at a very modest scale, less than a quarter of what another doctor would charge. It's just that you got into the habit of ignoring them.

Cousin Stanley: Maybe they went to the office and I didn't see them.

Mrs. Bird: They've always been sent to your home. And now I expect you to close the account; otherwise I'll have to take the usual steps.

Cousin Stanley: But half of Stoverville owed Lawson money, and *all* the family.

Mrs. Bird: The family *is* half of Stoverville. I can't write off all those accounts. You aren't related to me except by marriage.
Drop in a quick CU *of Christine, who is in the hall listening to this with much pleasure.*

Cousin Stanley: I won't pay. I can't pay.

Mrs. Bird: You'll have to come into court to explain why. I tell you, Stanley, this money is half of what Lawson left me, and I intend to preserve it and pass it on to Christine and her husband. And their children. If you want to know, it was Uncle Lou who advised me to take the matter into court. He paid Lawson's bills the same day he got them.

Cousin Stanley: Very well, I'll pay, but that's the last you'll ever see of me. (*He stomps out of the room, to the front door, flings it open, and leaves. We see bright shafts of sunshine through the wide doorway.*)

CUT TO:

SCENE 8: INTERNAL SEQUENCE. DAY. HALLWAY IN BIRD HOUSE.
Christine and Mrs. Bird hugging each other in the hallway with sunlight falling on them. Because of her pregnancy, Christine seems less agile and quick than her mother.

Christine: Hooray, oh boy, hooray. I've been waiting for that for years. It'll get around too.

Mrs. Bird: It just wasn't fair, Christine. Your father treated Stanley's family for years and never got paid one cent for his pains. I'll collect that money, you just wait and see.

Christine: Don't worry about passing it on to us, either. Spend it on yourself.

Mrs. Bird: I'd like for you and Jim and your children . . . (*She caresses Christine's belly lovingly.*)

(*TIGHT TWO-SHOT of mother and daughter. We get a strong sense of their resemblance and their love for one another.*)

. . . to have something from your father and me. Perhaps a down payment on a house. . . .

Christine: Mother, are you trying to sell me a house?
They are both laughing.

Mrs. Bird: It would keep the commission in the family.

Christine: I see I can go back to Montreal without worrying. You're going to be all right.

Mrs. Bird: Better than all right. Much much better than just "all right". I'm going to have my life.

CUT TO:

*SCENE 9: MONTAGE SEQUENCE. EXTERNAL AND IN-
TERNAL SEQUENCES.*
Brisk "doing business" MUSIC. *No dialogue. Only natural* SOUND
*of mallet, footsteps, car, voices in distance. We see Mrs. Bird's
hands and forearms holding a realtor's sign which says* SAMPSON
WILLEY REALTY, STOVERVILLE. FOR SALE. *She plants the sign in the
ground by its sharpened stake-end and pounds the flat end energetically with a mallet. Then we see Mrs. Bird escorting a young couple
up the walk of the house in whose front lawn the sign is standing.
Then we get a very* SHORT SHOT *of Mrs. Bird sitting at a desk in
an office with a typewriter in front of her. She is wearing a hat, and
picking out letters on the typewriter slowly, then faster, then faster
still. Finally we see a car bumping along very quickly over a back
concession road. It turns in to a farmhouse gate, stops, and Mrs.
Bird gets out. Passing some stray chickens and the farmhouse dog,
she disappears into a barn. She has a second realtor's sign under her
arm. In a moment she emerges from the barn with an elderly farmer
trotting along behind her.*

CUT TO:

*SCENE 10: INTERNAL SEQUENCE. DAY. THE OFFICE OF
WILLEY REALTY.*
*We are in a new set, the office of Willey Realty. Couple of desks,
filing cabinets. Through an open door we can see a receptionist's
desk. General air of modest but consistent success; the office is a
small but going concern.*

Mrs. Solomons: . . . and I got a letter from Sam this morning. He
likes it better in Montreal now, but I guess you know all about
that because he's Christine's obstetrician. When's the baby due,
by the way?

Mrs. Bird: I think about two months.

Mrs. Solomons: Don't you know for sure?

Mrs. Bird: I've been rushed to death in the office. You know, Naomi,
there's an awful lot to learn in this business. I've been at it since
last fall, and I haven't actually closed a sale.

Mrs. Solomons: What, not even one?

Mrs. Bird: Not actually closed one by myself, no, but I've passed
my exam, and I'm a certified salesperson.

Mrs. Solomons: When will you start actually earning money?

Mrs. Bird: Pretty soon now, I think. You're the first prospect I've had that looked like really doing business. You don't need that big place any more, now the children are grown up. If I can sell it for you and find you a smaller home, you'll be my first sale, and that'll get me rolling.

Mrs. Solomons: I didn't realize you were counting on us so much. I'm sorry I've taken up so much of your time with looking.

Mrs. Bird: That's what I'm here for, Naomi. Now, let's do some business. What about that town house in the east end? I tell you what, dear, I really think that's the house for you. Perfect for an older couple, and you could always use the second bedroom for a guest room. Suppose I put my hat on, and we go over and take another look.

Mrs. Solomons: I don't need to see it again, Ruth.

Mrs. Bird: Didn't you like it at all?

Mrs. Solomons: Oh yes, Ben and I both just loved it.

Mrs. Bird: It's perfect for you, in my opinion.

Mrs. Solomons: We're going to take it.

Mrs. Bird: Why, that's marvellous. My first sale. I'll fill out an offer.

Mrs. Solomons: We've already made an offer.

Mrs. Bird: No you haven't. I didn't file an offer for you.

Mrs. Solomons: Well . . . actually . . . Mr. Willey came by on Saturday and talked it over with us. He said there was no point in waiting any longer and he took us over to the development office and we made an offer on the spot. Twenty-six thousand.

Mrs. Bird: But you were my customer.

Mrs. Solomons: He just pushed us into it. You'll share the commission, isn't that right?

Mrs. Bird: Not if Sampson writes the offer and handles the closing. I guess I'm right out of it.

Mrs. Solomons: Oh, Ruth, I'm really sorry. I'll have Ben speak to Mr. Willey about the commission.   CUT TO:

SCENE 11: INTERNAL SEQUENCE. DAY. THE WILLEY REALTY OFFICE.

Mrs. Bird: . . . my first customers that looked anywhere ready to buy and you stole them away from me . . . and I've had others not so far along that you took over. I didn't mind at first because I thought you were trying to help me close the deal. But you've never once put my name on the offer. Am I just in the office to find prospects for you? I have to clothe myself, Mr. Willey, please remember that, and run my car and pay for my advertisements. I haven't cost you a cent, and you've made plenty of money from my getting out and digging. I want you to share the commission on the Solomons sale with me.

Willey: You want to know something, Ruth? Ben and Naomi were fed up with being shown house after house. They were ready to deal but you had them all confused. They'd seen a dozen houses and according to you every one was the best buy in Stoverville.

Mrs. Bird: When I'm showing a house I try to feel it's the best property in town. You told me to do that yourself.

Willey: I know I did, but you haven't got the feel of it yet. You have to make it like a story, like a little play. You have to sense how close the prospect is to a commitment. I've seen you waste two or three days on prospects I knew weren't serious.

Mrs. Bird: But the Solomons were serious and I knew it.

Willey: You were losing them. You were letting them off the hook.

Mrs. Bird: No, I was trying to be——

Willey: Don't interrupt me, let me finish, or you'll never be worth a damn in real estate. Every sale has its own rhythm and its own pace and story. You have to know exactly when to move in. You've got to sock it to them and make them like it. If you lose the rhythm, you'll lose your confidence and you'll never make the sale.

Mrs. Bird: The fact remains that you stole my client.

Willey: You were *losing* them. In a week they'd have gone to somebody else. I was a pal of Lawson's, sure, but in this office I'm doing business, and I won't let you cost me a chance to do business.

Mrs. Bird: That's heartless. It's mean.

Willey: Ruth, grow up! This isn't your nice big old home on Charleston Road. This is the world!

TIGHT CLOSE-UP *of Mrs. Bird*

Mrs. Bird: It's hard. It's hard.

Willey: Life is hard. Next time I see you backing off on a sale, I'll grab it just the same.

Mrs. Bird: I could take you before the Real Estate Board.

Willey: They'll tell you exactly what I've just told you. Be careful not to make yourself into a joke.

Mrs. Bird: Right. Right! As long as I'm working out of this office, I'll keep my clients out of your way, and if I get a chance to steal any of yours. I'll do it.

Willey: *(Big grin on his face)* You're welcome to try but you haven't got a chance. And if you think I'm crooked, wait till you run up against the other bastards in town. They'll skin you alive.

Mrs. Bird: Not after this they won't.

FADE OUT.

END OF ACT TWO

ACT THREE

FADE IN:

SCENE 12: INTERNAL SEQUENCE. EVENING.

This short scene is supposed to be in Jim and Christine's apartment in Montreal, but the designer can simply re-dress a corner of the set from the first act, the Bird house in Stoverville. We hear very occasional baby cries and gurglings through this scene, just enough to establish, not enough to get a laugh. We are watching Jim and Christine as they read over a letter from Mrs. Bird.

Jim: Quick, what does she say? Where are we going to put her? I was hoping she wouldn't come till we get the baby off the two A.M. feeding. I hate having him in our room.

Christine: He can go into the living room.

Jim: But then it's such a mess in the morning. What does she say?

Christine: *(Reading)* ". . . and I left Willey because he was cheating me over every sale. What a bandit! But Mr. **Langbourne** was down from London last week, and I talked him into taking me into the Stoverville branch. They have branches all over Ontario, so it looks like a real opportunity. I expect to make my first independent sale this week. You've got to sock it to them and make them swallow it. You can't let them off the hook."

Jim and Christine stare at each other.

Jim: That doesn't sound like your mother.

Christine: *(Still reading)* ". . . this man Szekely came to Stoverville about a year ago. There are a number of people from Hungary working up at the plant, and all over town. He buys houses and fixes them up for rooming houses and flats and rents them to the Hungarians. I brought him into the office . . ."

Jim: Doesn't she say anything about the baby?

Christine: Not one word.

Jim: That's not like her either.

Christine: She never used to miss a chance to see us.

CUT TO:

SCENE 13: INTERNAL SEQUENCE. DAY. LARGE MODERN REAL-ESTATE OFFICE.

This is the last full set needed for production of the play: a large ultra-modern real-estate office with a wide plate-glass window out front with lettering: LANGBOURNE ASSOCIATES: REAL ESTATE: MORTGAGES! TORONTO, LONDON, PETERBOROUGH, STOVERVILLE. *We should be able to watch mimed action through this window. At the beginning of the scene, however, we are inside the office watching Mrs. Bird on the phone.*

Mrs. Bird: *(Energetically, into the phone)* . . . no, no. No! No, I tell you, there's not the slightest use your coming into the office unless you've got some money. It's a waste of both our time. . . . You do? . . . Oh, you do? . . . How much? Where did you get it? . . . What do you have to pay on it? . . . What? . . . You can't carry a second mortgage on your salary. . . . What? Oh, I see. Yes, if you could arrange that, we might talk business. If he didn't charge you interest. Then you could carry the first mortgage. You could handle it that way, but otherwise we can't do a thing for you. All right. That's right. Call me back.

During this speech, the office manager, Larry Godfrey, enters. He stands watching Mrs. Bird closely. She waves her pencil back and forth at him as she talks. He speaks when she hangs up.

Godfrey: Hitchcock?

Mrs. Bird: He says his grandfather might put up the down payment.

Godfrey: I thought for sure you were wasting your time over the place. It's been listed for two years.

Mrs. Bird: His wife keeps bugging him. She's a friend of my daughter's. She can see the intangibles.

Godfrey: Do you think they'll go for it?

Mrs. Bird: They'll have to get the money from the old man. Then we'll see.

Godfrey: You know, when I was transferred from Toronto I was depressed about it. I didn't know eastern Ontario at all, and no matter how much you go out looking at properties you just can't get to know the region in a couple of years.

Mrs. Bird: I can tell you all you need to know. Before I got into this business, I did nothing but study this town and the people.

Godfrey: If you can make this Hitchcock sale, you'll have me convinced.

Mrs. Bird: That reminds me, I've got to call the trust company about the Hitchcock mortgage. We really should have our own mortgage department.

Godfrey: We do, in Toronto, London, and Peterborough. I guess Mr. Langbourne thinks we aren't quite ready.

Mrs. Bird: We're losing clients that way, and why should the trust company collect interest, instead of us?

Godfrey: Do you think we're doing a big enough volume?

Mrs. Bird: If we aren't now, we soon will be. Anyway, the mortgage department can wait. After I phone the trust, I've got to write up the new Szekely papers. He's going to offer for all three properties in a package deal. . . .

(Cousin Stanley slinks into the office, looking somewhat abashed. Godfrey is clearly not much impressed by his appearance or manner.)

. . . why, hello there, Stanley, have you met our new manager? Mr. Godfrey—Mr. Bird.

Godfrey: How do you do, Mr. Bird. Can we interest you in anything?

Cousin Stanley: Not today, thanks. I'm not in the market. In fact I'm selling.

Godfrey smiles politely and exits. TWO-SHOT *of Stanley and Mrs. Bird.*

Mrs. Bird: Did you want to see me about something, Stanley?

Cousin Stanley: *(Embarrassed, as well he might be)* The fact is, Ruth, I've got to do something about my mortgage. I've always used the house equity to finance inventory at the showroom, but now the payments have gotten out of hand.

Mrs. Bird: I told you that months ago, Stanley. What you really should do is get rid of that big place and take a low-rent apartment. That would reduce your upkeep costs and expenses close to five hundred a month.

Cousin Stanley: But how would it look?

Mrs. Bird: You can't keep up appearances in Bankruptcy Court, Stanley. Why don't you put yourself in my hands? I've got an idea about that place of yours. We just might move it to an institution or a funeral director.

Cousin Stanley: No possible way. The zoning forbids it.

Mrs. Bird: The zoning is not a serious problem . . . *(There is a pause while they eye each other warily.)* . . . come on now, Stanley, aren't you going to try to sell me a car?

Cousin Stanley: Lawson got a real good deal on the car you've been driving.

Mrs. Bird: I've had good use out of it, Stanley, there's no denying.

Cousin Stanley: Now you need a new car, I hope you'll come to me. I've got a steel-grey demonstrator that would just suit you.

Mrs. Bird: No, I'll tell you what I have in mind. A pickup.

Cousin Stanley: A pickup?

Mrs. Bird: An extended-cab pickup, one of the big ones with the picture rear-window and four-wheel drive. I get over some mighty rough roads in the back concessions. I'll try to work you in on the sale if I can. Maybe you can unload my present car. . . .

CUT TO:

SCENE 14: INTERNAL SEQUENCE. NIGHT. THE LANG-BOURNE OFFICE.
We are in the large office quite late at night. There is a single pool of light over the desk Mrs. Bird uses, and we have the sense of plenty

of dark space around her. A conspiratorial air to the whole scene. It is a key scene, and Mrs. Bird's long speech at the end is the most important speech in the play and needs to be brilliantly acted. The model for the speech is the second-act closing speech of Pinter's The Caretaker, *where Aston explains how he underwent electric shock therapy. The speech should be delivered haltingly, almost musingly. It has a strong feminist flavour, but paradoxically is almost perfect Christian sacramental theology on marriage.*

Mrs. Bird: Put your signature there, and there, Andras, and I'll get it into the Seymour office first thing tomorrow. You'll make money on this purchase.

Szekely: I know.

Mrs. Bird: You don't leave much to chance.

Szekely: Chance is a luxury I cannot afford. Long before I tried to get out of Hungary I had funds to my credit in Switzerland. It wasn't easy to transfer the money. One man who carried drafts for me is still in prison. Another has been searching for his wife and children all over Europe for a decade. I try not to leave anything to chance.

Mrs. Bird: You must have seen some very sad things.

Szekely: I have . . . children starving . . . men shot for no reason . . . I won't go on with it, but, you see, I like a little security. Property in my name. Friends who can count on me. I've done well since I came to Canada. I've got tenants ready to fill these houses. *(He indicates the papers he is in process of signing.)* I'll make money while I'm paying for them, and I'll amass more capital for investment. You have to care for yourself in this world; nobody will do it for you.

Mrs. Bird: My husband took pretty good care of me.

Szekely: I've heard he left you only a small inheritance.

Mrs. Bird: It wasn't enough to live on, but it was money. I've been able to add to it. Now it's a respectable sum. I might do something with it in mortgages.

Szekely: You mean you've got between twenty and twenty-five thousand.

Mrs. Bird: A very good guess.

Szekely: I don't guess, Mrs. Bird.

Mrs. Bird: No, I suppose not.

Szekely: Twenty thousand dollars . . . or a bit more . . . is not a big sum, but it isn't negligible. There are things one could do with it, maybe by adding it in with other holdings. I'm not a great capitalist myself.

Mrs. Bird: How much have you to spare?

Szekely: Ah, that would be telling . . . but you are welcome to guess.

Mrs. Bird: Free at this moment, and ready to put into new properties? I'd say around thirty-five thousand or a shade more.

They both laugh; they enjoy each other's company.

Szekely: That's why I like doing business with you, Ruth. You don't waste time over inessentials. So . . . what about it?

Mrs. Bird: What about what?

Szekely: Should we go in together? We can do much more with sixty thousand than we could separately. You want to sell me that enormous house of your cousin Stanley, correct?

Mrs. Bird: I think we could do something with the property that Stanley hasn't the initiative to see. It's a perfect location.

Szekely: For a riverfront hotel, perhaps?

Mrs. Bird: And a marina, that's an essential.

Szekely: It would require more capital than I can manage at present. Why not come in with me . . . as a permanent arrangement?

Mrs. Bird: What sort of arrangement?

Szekely: The usual one. A marriage contract. Your property would be completely safeguarded.

Mrs. Bird: You mean you'd like us to get married?

Szekely: It's the best way to manage this affair.

Mrs. Bird: That's very sensible of you, Andras, and very kind.

Szekely: Kindness has very little to do with it.

Mrs. Bird: I think it has. I'll tell you something, Andras, that I wouldn't say to anyone else. Lawson was a very selfish man. Yes, he was. An extremely selfish man. Everybody thought he was a darling, but he had all the life and I had none. I stayed home and listened to the neighbours and all our friends and relations singing his praises . . . my own family was off at the other end of Ontario and in time they died and I had no family but his . . . and to them

I was always an outsider. . . . *(She takes a bit of a pause here. Camera comes in for* CLOSE-UP *on her bare, un-madeup middle-aged face. We want utter simplicity here!)* But I'll tell you something strange, Andras. Lawson was selfish and inconsiderate and foolish and improvident, but I loved him. I can't explain that. I just did. *(There should be the feeling of great loneliness and loss in her face here.)* In many ways he was an impossible man; sometimes he didn't seem to know I was a living person . . . he never talked to me very much. But he wasn't deliberately unkind. He just went ahead and did what he thought was right. He was not a great doctor, but his patients had confidence in him and they mostly got well. They took their life from him, and when they called for him, he always came . . . and then he was such a kind father. I don't know how it is. A lot of girls and women these days aren't interested in being married; they're afraid of just that kind of servitude. Perhaps rightly. I can't say. When you've been married, the way I was married, it marks you, and you can't do it a second time. I couldn't ever feel married to anybody else, even on a business basis.

Szekely: Very well, if that's how you feel, perhaps we can work out something else almost as suitable.

Mrs. Bird: You're not too upset?

Szekely: *(Smiles.)* I'm past fifty, Ruth. I've been disappointed before.

FADE OUT.

END OF ACT THREE

ACT FOUR

FADE IN:

SCENE 15: INTERNAL SEQUENCE. DAY. LANGBOURNE REALTY OFFICE.

We open with a SHOT *through the plate-glass window of the office, watching Mrs. Bird—in mime—scolding Cousin Stanley energetically. Then we appear to move in through the window until we are in a medium-close* TWO-SHOT.

Mrs. Bird: Stanley, Stanley, what's going to become of you? I've told you a thousand times there's nothing to be gained by coming back at me with this. When you owned the house, you had exactly the same opportunity to develop it.

Cousin Stanley: Where would I ever get the money that's gone into renovation and promotion and equipment? Electric signs! You and Szekely cheated me out of the chance, Ruth.

Mrs. Bird: Nonsense! All you ever did with the house was live in it and use it to secure loans. Why, you begged me to sell it for you.

Cousin Stanley: It was your idea to sell it, not mine. Why didn't you ask me to go in with you?

Mrs. Bird: You just said yourself you had no money. It had to be done by somebody like Andras Szekely, with drive and motivation. He's got a gold mine there. PANNONIA MARINE WONDERLAND. FINE FOOD. OVERNIGHT ACCOMMODATION. MARINA. THOUSAND ISLANDS TOURS . . .

Cousin Stanley: There's something else that annoys me. What is this Pannonia stuff, anyway?

Mrs. Bird: That's just the Latin word for Hungary.

Cousin Stanley: Latin, Hungary. I saw a car with an Arkansas plate parked there this morning, and it's your fault. You let that house go out of the family.

Mrs. Bird: Not right out. I'm holding a one-third interest.

Cousin Stanley: Why you lucky . . . woman! *(He spits this last word out.)*

Mrs. Bird: Luck had nothing to do with it; it was planning. Thanks to Andras and me a lot of people will make money out of it. It's just a small operation now, but we're going to put the earnings back into expansion. We'll add another motel wing and increase the overnight accommodation. We'll extend the marina. Maybe in a couple of summers we'll set up our own yacht club.

Cousin Stanley: You've had to cut some pretty sharp corners. I wouldn't want it on my conscience.

Mrs. Bird: You mean the zoning regulations? Why, for years the town has been wailing about low assessments in the east end. Now we're assessed at four times what you were. When we appeared before the zoning committee, they had the good sense to see it—Uncle Lou, Jack Sniderman, and one or two others.

Cousin Stanley: But you did your renovating and applied for a liquor licence *before* you went to city council. How come you were so sure you were going to be re-zoned?

Mrs. Bird: Stop acting like a prosecuting attorney, Stanley. I wouldn't do anything wrong, and you know it. All we did was check on what property the councilmen owned. Then we showed them how increased assessment could work for all of us in Stoverville.

Cousin Stanley: What's good for Andras Szekely is good for Stoverville.

Mrs. Bird: There's plenty of truth in that. We could use more like him.

Cousin Stanley: Coming in here and taking our jobs.

Mrs. Bird: You're acting mighty tiresome today, Stanley. Did you come in just to gossip and pass backchat?

Cousin Stanley: I came to do business. In some ways, I'm glad you got me out of that house, although I wish I'd been in on the renovation. Still, I've been able to cut back expenses, like you said, and I'm not in the hole I've been in the last couple of years. This year's models are going well . . . fairly well, anyway.

Mrs. Bird: So now you want to go into a new house, have me find you a top-quality deal, waive my commission, and get you the best possible mortgage terms.

Cousin Stanley: How did you know?

Mrs. Bird: Stanley . . . Stanley . . . Stanley . . .

Cousin Stanley: All right, all right *(Laughing grudgingly)* but will you do it?

Mrs. Bird: I'll tell you what I'm going to do. I'll find you a good solid small house, nothing undignified—you can count on that—and I'll get you a mortgage that doesn't drive you into the ground.

She is being quite nice to him; we want to establish believable human conduct. She is very willing to try to get along with people like Stanley. And he is rather overwhelmed by this.

Cousin Stanley: That's damned thoughtful of you, Ruth, and I appreciate it.

Mrs. Bird: When the time comes for me and Andras to look for fresh capital, if you've got a few thousand you want to risk at that time, I'll work you in, so you won't feel your old house has gone right away from you. *(Smiling)* I don't want to cheat you, Stanley, or be your enemy. I just want to be your equal.

CUT TO:

SCENE 16: INTERNAL SEQUENCE. DAY. THE LANG-BOURNE OFFICE.
This is Mrs. Bird's big triumphal scene, with plenty of comic under-tones. Uncle Lou, Sampson Willey, Larry Godfrey, in conversation. Office workers busy in background. A good deal of "busy-busy" business, typewriters, phones.

Godfrey: *(To Willey)* Stop peeking at the filing cabinets, Sampson, you'll get nothing out of them.

Willey: What have you got in here, now, eight salesmen?

Godfrey: Ten, not counting myself and Ruth Bird. She's technically the office manager. I'm the branch manager, but we both spend most of our time selling. We've got a girl on the switchboard and a couple of clerks too.

Willey: You must be as big as the other Langbourne branches, right?

Godfrey: Not as big as Toronto or London, but I think we're about even with Peterborough.

Uncle Lou: What is it, three years you've been here now?

Godfrey: We came here just about the time Sampson let Ruth go.

Willey: *(Sharply)* I didn't let her go. She quit on me.

Uncle Lou: That makes it four years since Lawson Bird died. It doesn't seem that long.

Willey keeps prowling around looking at stuff. He spots a wall chart.

Willey: I was in the boat with him when he died . . . what's this, your sales graph?

Godfrey: Keeps going up.

Willey: And you're doing mortgage financing too?

Godfrey: That was Ruth's idea.

Willey: Ruth, Ruth, Ruth. I never thought I'd be coming over here with this. *(He takes an envelope and a scroll from his briefcase.)*

Godfrey: Who's making the presentation?

Willey: *(To Uncle Lou)* You are, you're the Mayor.

Godfrey: How does the Mayor come into it?

Willey: Well, you have to figure that real estate is tied up with Stoverville's development. The realtors really shape the town, *(Giving Uncle Lou a sidelong look)* sometimes in ways you might not expect.

Uncle Lou: *(Deliberately)* Like that deal of yours with the super-market chain from Ottawa.

Godfrey: An occasional stretching doesn't hurt anybody. If you're too inflexible about building regulations, you get a stagnant climate.

We see Mrs. Bird through the window in a reversal of the SHOT. *She enters the office from the street. She calls as she comes in.*

Mrs. Bird: Okay, if you want to go to lunch, Larry.

Godfrey: I'll just stick around for the ceremony.

Mrs. Bird: *(Eyeing Willey)* What ceremony? What are you doing here, Sampson? At this very moment you're supposed to be in Bert Leventritt's office, telling him the frontage I proposed isn't enough and that you've got a better spot out by Highway 401.

Willey: How do you know?

Mrs. Bird: I just came from there. He said you were coming in at noon. I'm afraid you'll be out of luck there, Sampson. We fixed it up before lunch.

Willey: Well, damn you anyway . . . *(A pause. The other men try to restrain their laughter.)* . . . I tell you guys, this woman is capable of anything. *(To Mrs. Bird)* I suppose you've got the whole scheme set up by now.

Mrs. Bird: Just about wrapped up.

Willey: *(Severely)* Ruth, that was my customer.

Mrs. Bird: Where have I heard that tune before?

Willey: I ought to report you to the Grievance Committee.

Mrs. Bird: Wouldn't do you a bit of good.

Willey: I know.

Mrs. Bird: *(To Godfrey)* I hope you haven't been letting Sampson snoop around, Larry.

Godfrey: I've been keeping an eye on him.

Uncle Lou: *(Hilarious)* God, Ruthie, you're a terror.

Willey: All right, let's cut out the joking and get on with it.

Mrs. Bird: This is where we really have to watch him, Larry.

Willey: Cut it out, now, or I won't give you the money.

Mrs. Bird: What money? Oh, oh . . . I see. The award. I'm afraid I haven't been keeping track of the listings lately. Too much on my mind.

Willey: How many times a day does she check them, Larry?

Godfrey: Never more than fifty.

The three men take a more formal attitude.

Willey: About what I figured. *(To Mrs. Bird)* You know, I'm President of the Real Estate Board this year, Ruth, and Lou is Mayor, so you can see for yourself why we're here. This is the end of the second quarter—April, May, June, the best months of the year. In aggregate sales for this quarter, your name leads all the rest. You're well out in front. Larry is in third spot, and I'm right back of him . . . and what the hell, we've had our differences, Ruth, and I'll grab your clients whenever I've got the chance . . . but all the same . . .

Godfrey: I'm keeping my eye on him from now on, Ruth. . . .

Willey: . . . and much as I hate to admit it, you're a born salesman . . . or should I say salesperson . . . anyway, whatever, you're it.

Mrs. Bird: Any hard feelings, Sampson?

Willey: Just a few. It's those lost commissions. But as this year's President, I'm here to present you with our Bonus Listings Award for the second quarter, a cheque for five hundred dollars, and this handsomely lithographed scroll. I'm not going to claim it makes me very happy because it doesn't, it's costing me money. But there it is, you won it.

Mrs. Bird: That speech does you credit, Sampson.

Uncle Lou: *(Giving Ruth a hug and a kiss)* At this point I usually say a few words, but I'll skip it this time. It's five hundred dollars in found money, Ruth, and I hope you spend it on yourself.

Mrs. Bird: I'm so pleased I don't know what to say.

Godfrey: You've got a great future.

Mrs. Bird: Imagine! A fifty-five-year-old widow with a great future.
CUT TO:

SCENE 17: INTERNAL SEQUENCE. NIGHT. JIM AND CHRISTINE'S APARTMENT, MONTREAL.
Jim and Christine in a tight TWO-SHOT. *As before, the designer may merely re-dress a corner of the first-act set for this short scene. Christine has just opened a letter. She takes out a small slip of paper.*

Jim: I hope that's what it seems to be.

Christine: It's a cheque all right . . . for five hundred dollars.

Jim: A present for us? What does she say?

Christine: *(Reading the letter)* "Dear kids: I'm sorry I won't get to see you while I'm in Montreal. The convention runs three days, and it's taking all my time, and I still haven't met my grandchild. I know it's awful, but these days I have to attend strictly to business. Tomorrow night I'm going to dinner at Chez Bardet with Mr. Godfrey, and in the afternoon I'm addressing the convention on the subject of 'The Woman Realtor'. I hope the enclosed cheque will help make my apologies. From now on, I'll be able to help you more than I ever hoped. Meanwhile, take care of yourselves and the baby. Your loving Mom."

Jim looks hungrily at the cheque.

Jim: She's in Montreal, and she isn't coming to see us?

Christine: *(A little sadly)* So she says.

Jim: I never heard of such a thing.

CUT TO:

SCENE 18: INTERNAL SEQUENCE. NIGHT. MONTREAL RESTAURANT.
This scene might be done very simply with a table and chairs and fittings, or if money is available it can be done on location, or a set can be built. It is a very very fancy Montreal restaurant; there could be a crowd of diners, if the producer wants it. This is the apotheosis of Mrs. Bird. She wears a very tasteful, obviously expensive, cocktail dress. New coiffure. Her clothes have been gradually changing throughout the play. Now she looks wonderful. The whole point of the scene can be made visually.

Godfrey: *(Very confidential, leaning on heavily laden table)* I could see you were going to be one of the great ones as soon as Langbourne brought you into the office, and there's no reason at all why he should get a cut from everything we do. Have you ever thought of opening your own office? Godfrey and Bird? Or else Bird and Godfrey, if you like that better. We could go a long way together.

Mrs. Bird: Oh no, not you too.

Godfrey: What?

Mrs. Bird: Nothing . . . nothing . . . I was thinking out loud.

Godfrey: Let me give you some more wine. *(They drink.)* I never heard a better address than the one you gave this afternoon. I'm going to propose a toast . . . To future prospects.

Mrs. Bird: *(Raising her glass)* To future prospects.

Godfrey: We can take the whole office staff with us. They all feel the same way.

Mrs. Bird: But we won't do anything mean . . . or disloyal . . . will we?

Godfrey: I should say not! Here, tell you what we do. There's a good storefront on King Street, just needs a certain amount of paint, plenty of staff room. We'll move in there as soon as we can arrange things . . .

His voice fades slowly. The camera DOLLIES BACK *as they continue their planning, until we have a wide view of this splendid room.*

FADE OUT.

The Man from Inner Space

Eric Nicol

Richard Savage

The Man from Inner Space

Eric Nicol

Characters

DAVID SLOAN a public-relations man in his forties
JOAN a girl in her twenties
ROBBIE a young thug

ACT ONE

FADE IN:

SCENE 1:
VIDEO:
AERIAL FILM *or* STILL *of Vancouver's West End, specifically the high-rise apartment buildings that have turned this part of the city into one of Canada's most densely populated areas. Not a glamour shot. If possible, rain and low cloud.*
Time: Dusk. As the camera moves in on the scene:
SOUND:
The urban blight of a mélange of car horns, emergency vehicle siren, float plane (prop) engine, traffic roar, and angry voices, crescendo and out with:

CUT TO:

VIDEO:

Lobby of one of the apartment buildings, as David enters, the door closing off the noise, which is replaced with:

MUSIC:

The piped, bland-leading-the-bland burble with which office and residential buildings sedate the transient.

VIDEO:

Titles, over David furling his wet umbrella. David: in his forties. Physically undistinguished, on the short side, the owner of the kind of face and form that light a fire only in women with a low threshold of combustion. He is a loser, in the Inspector Clouseau tradition, but only in so far as the Edsel belongs to the same family as the bath-chair. He has refined the technique of losing. For example, he has trained his mouth to wear a small smile at all times in public, a smile that suggests that he has private information that he is a success. The rest of his body, its movement and gestures, and especially his eyes, contradict the smile. Yet as a loser he has a winning quality: he has desire. If at first he succeeds, he'll try, try again.

These traits are illustrated by the initial episode in the lobby of the apartment buildings. David, who is wearing old jeans, a Cowichan Indian sweater, and a black homburg, and carries a fat briefcase, has done a neat job of furling his rain-soaked umbrella. He notices the parched rubber plant in its pot. He shakes the excess moisture from the umbrella on the plant, vigorously, and in so doing shears off the unhappy plant's one remaining large shoot.

SOUND:

At once, the piped music is overlaid by the traffic roar and the police siren. Which subside with:

VIDEO:

David looks at the entrance in time to see the door closing. Someone has left the building while he was maiming the rubber plant. He claws a hole in the hard earth of the pot and inserts the broken shoot, patting the dry dirt around it. As a final benison he shakes the remaining drops of water from his homburg on the shoot. It falls over.

David picks up the briefcase and umbrella and enters the elevator.

CUT TO:

*SCENE 2: INTERNAL SEQUENCE. INTERIOR OF ELE-
VATOR.*
*The furled umbrella resting on his shoulder, David gazes for a
moment at the floor buttons, then responds to the challenge: he
salutes his opponent with the foil, moves it through the en garde
position, and lunges. CU of the point just missing button 8 once,
button 8 twice, then hitting squarely—the emergency button. The
alarm bell rings wildly. Still clinging to his cool, David walks out
of the elevator to the stairs, en route stepping carefully over the
felled shoot of the rubber plant.*

CUT TO:

SCENE 3: INTERNAL SEQUENCE. DOOR OF APARTMENT.
*David emerges from the stairwell, having climbed the eight floors.
He walks to an apartment door, knocks on it, and waits. He knocks
a second time, then puts a key in the lock, opens the door, and enters
the flat.*

CUT TO:

SCENE 4: INTERNAL SEQUENCE. INSIDE OF APARTMENT.
*David has flattened himself beside the doorway, leaving the door
open.*

David: Okay. I know you're in here. And I know you're desperate.
I also know that you are a fellow human being, forced to resort
to burglary by circumstances beyond your control. To avoid
bloodshed, I am leaving the door open for five seconds, to give
you a chance to escape with dignity, no questions asked. If instead you choose to remain, you will be trapped with a person
who has no fear of death, being afflicted with a terminal disease.

*David waits five seconds, then moves cautiously, alert, mission-
impossible, to the console of a stereo record and cassette player.
CU his index finger pushing the "play" button.*
MUSIC:
*The piped music is abruptly buried under "My Favorite Things",
the Julie Andrews vocal. Behind:*

> *David quickly returns to the door, closes it, secures the Yale lock,
> inserts the chain lock, pushes home the bolt, and places an iron bar
> resting on the floor against the door.*

> *He goes to the French doors leading to the sundeck, and draws
> the drapes to exclude the outside world and its light. He turns and
> surveys the flat, the large living room of which is furnished with:*

an old-fashioned roll-top desk and swivel chair
an elaborate stereo sound system
a large screen set up for back projection of film
a small, round café table with two wicker chairs
a stationary bicycle
a rowing machine
a casket, in which are stored props and costumes
a small aquarium, inhabited by one goldfish
The Pullman kitchen, a bedroom, and a bathroom complete David's accommodation.

Above a small bookshelf on one wall hangs a three-foot totem pole, with the raven at the bottom, on whose beak David hangs the umbrella and the homburg. He carries the briefcase to the table, opens it, and takes out a package of frozen food, from which he removes the wrapper. He carries the tray to the aquarium and addresses the goldfish.

David: Good evening, Sarah. Guess what we have for dinner tonight! No, not frozen ant eggs. No, not chopped worm Alsacienne. It's something for *me*! Frozen Swiss fondue! Tonight is Switzerland Night. How does *that* grab your gills?

MUSIC:
Segues into another melody from The Sound of Music.

Humming along with the music, David checks the pre-set heat, sets timer, and pops the fondue into the oven. He returns to his briefcase and extracts a rented can of film, whose title is seen in CU: Glories of the Alps. *During this:*

David: What kind of an afternoon did you have, Sarah? Whadya mean, you've been cooped up all day? You don't know how lucky you are, in that nice, comparatively dry tank. Baby, it's Vancouver *raining* out there. And it isn't raining rain you know, it's raining moisturized pollution. Bad! I had to stand and wait for a traffic light, and one guy from the federal Department of the Environment came along and tried to staple a sign to me saying that Granville Street was too polluted for swimming. *(He gets the film ready for the projector.)* But now we're home and dry, and ready for an evening of . . . holiday in Switzerland!

CLOSE-UP:

Sarah gaping.

What's that you say? Don't mumble, woman! If we're to have a meaningful relationship you must express your hostility openly and frankly. . . . Well, that's more like it. You don't want to holiday in Switzerland. You'd prefer an evening in Hawaii. Because you'd have a better chance of meeting a big, handsome sailfish.

During this exercise in communication David completes setting up the projector and opens the lid of the casket to take out his Swiss garb: colourful shirt, lederhosen, and sandals, and he starts to change.

David: No, no, I appreciate your being honest. But to be equally honest, Sarah, I'm surprised that you persist in these sexual fantasies of meeting a piscine Paul Newman. The water in your aquarium is filtered, temperature-controlled, with minimum risk of oil spill from a super-tanker. Yet you continue to hanker to swim in the notoriously filthy ocean in hopes of making it with some stud loaded with mercury. . . . All right! All right! You feel that I'm trying to manipulate you. I'd hoped that you would be able to distinguish between male domination and friendly advice offered by an intelligence that is superior, though only relatively. You are free to frolic off Waikiki. Me, I'm off to the land that has the world's largest known reserves of cool . . .

David rowing on the Lake of Geneva. After a moment of plying the oars in blissful enjoyment of the backdrop of mountain and lake, he pauses to unwrap a triangular bar of Tobler chocolate, breaking off a segment neatly and nibbling it with great satisfaction.

David: Dear Sarah: you should have come to Switzerland with me. Happiness is boating on the Lake of Geneva. This country really turns me on. *(Inhales deeply.)* You can just *smell* the neutrality . . . the great Swiss talent for not becoming emotionally involved. These people know how to *survive,* Sarah. Locked in their little room in the mountains. What a triumph of isolation! They've taken themselves out of it, clean, clean, out of it. Magnificent!

MUSIC: *Changes to William Tell Overture.*

(David picks up the oars.) Time to be off, to see the castle of Chillon. You remember Byron's poem, Sarah? Who could forget those immortal lines . . . *(He picks up a book of verse and reads.)*

"Eternal Spirit of the chainless Mind!
Brightest in dungeons, Liberty, thou art—
For there thy habitation is the heart—"

SOUND: *A loud knock at the door.*

MUSIC: *Out.*

Film projector stopped. David stands at the door, listening.

SOUND: *The knock repeated.*

David removes the iron bar, unbolts and unlocks the door, leaving the chain on. He opens the door. Outside stands Joan. About 25. Attractive in a fresh-faced way, drawing on inner sources of beauty. She wears a white rain-hat and a white raincoat, carries a satchel full of copies of Signpost *magazine, and holds a clipboard on which to write names and addresses.*

Joan: Good evening. I'm here for the Crusaders for Christ, who are having our national rally here. Do you have a spare room you could rent to us?

David: A spare room? Good God, no. I'm full. That is, my *rooms* are full—of me. What I'm trying to say is, my rooms find me very filling, ha, ha. Sorry . . .

Joan: I understand. Have you seen this issue of *Signpost*? How we may attain salvation by the instrument of love. You——

David: No, thanks. I don't use it.

Joan: Don't use what?

David: Love. I tried it once, but I found that it was bad for my hands. *(He holds up hands as spastic clams.)* See, they still aren't quite right. Thanks for calling. *(David closes the door.)*

Joan: *(Outside)* Ow!

David opens the door. Joan, in pain, clutches the fingers he has caught in the door.

David: I caught your fingers in the door. I didn't need to. I just, stupidly, caught your fingers in the door.

Joan: It's all right.

David takes off the chain and opens the door wide.

David: No, it's not all right. I want to apologize, very sincerely, and I want you to know that I *am* covered by liability insurance.

(Joan is not comforted. A tear escapes her effort to contain the hurt.)

You're crying. No, no, you mustn't cry. Crying can have serious complications. . . . Please . . . come in.

(Joan shakes her head, but David guides her into the room.)

Please. Let me get something for your fingers. A Band-Aid, perhaps . . . no, something larger than a Band-Aid. Something to reduce the swelling . . . *(Noticing the snow-peaked mountain on which the projector stopped)* Ice! An ice pack! *(He goes to the fridge and removes the tray of ice cubes)* Ice cubes!

Joan: *(Disturbed by the strange décor)* Please don't bother. I can——

David: No bother. No bother at all. Ice cubes are available without a prescription. Now, how do we get them around those fingers? We need a mitt, a large mitt . . . eureka! *(He grabs an oven mitt from its hook above the stove.)*

Joan: No, please, I'm putting you to too much trouble . . .

David: *(Pouring ice cubes into oven mitt)* No trouble. No trouble at all. Now, if you wouldn't mind slipping this on, madam.

Joan: *(Putting the injured hand into the oven mitt)* Thank you. . . .

David: Perfect. Fits like a glove. *(Trying to usher her out)* Do come again.

Joan: I can't take your oven mitt.

David: Compliments of the chef. Really. We don't need an oven mitt. We never use the oven.

SOUND: *Buzzer of the oven timer.*

We hardly ever use the oven. Excuse me. *(He turns off the buzzer and the oven.)* My fondue is done.

Joan: Your what?

David: My Swiss fondue. You've had Swiss fondue.

Joan: What is it?

David: Swiss fondue . . . is cheese that has learned to go it alone.

Joan: May I try it?

David is appalled. As of now, when the camera cuts to Joan the door behind her is closed.

David: May you try it? But . . . what about your hand?

Joan: Oh, it feels much better, thanks.

David: Did you close the door?

Joan: No.

CLOSE-UP:

David's face.

David: No? . . . Then *I* must have.

CUT TO:

Joan sitting at the table, David placing the bowl of fondue before her.

MUSIC: *Reprise of* Glories of the Alps *background.*

Joan: Do you mind if I take off your oven mitt?

David: No. No, of course not.

Joan removes the oven mitt, putting it on the table, and also takes off her hat and coat. To David's alarm, she is wearing a colourful sweater and ski pants. On screen: Alpine Chalet Resort.

David: *(After the fact)* Take off your mitt . . . and your hat . . . and your coat. . . . Do you always wear that outfit?

Joan: No, just today. Aren't you going to join me?

David: That seems to be how it's developing. *(David sits down, taking from his breast pocket a pair of mirrored sunglasses and putting them on.)*

Joan: Mm, this is good. Do have some.

David: Thank you. *(Noting her expertise with the bread chunks)* You've eaten fondue before.

Joan: Oh, yes. But I didn't know it was Swiss. This is fun.

David: No, Miss . . . what is your name?

Joan: Joan.

David: You have a surname.

Joan: Mm. But I hardly ever use it. What's *your* name?

David: Sloan. Mr. Sloan.

Joan: Oh. What's your first name?

David: I don't have a first name. My family was very poor.

Joan: I think your first name is David.

David: What makes you think so?

Joan: I saw it on the letter box in the lobby. "David Sloan". You were going to tell me something, David.

David: I can't imagine what it would be.

Joan: About this not being fun.

David: Yes. I was going to tell you that this is fun, but not *just* fun.

Joan: Ah. This is how you *live*. How very, very interesting. I'd love to hear more about it, David. If you'd be kind enough to explain it to me.

David: I explained it to my mother. Why shouldn't I explain it to you?

Joan: Your mother lives with you?

David: No. She is having an affair with my father. In fact I believe they're married.

Joan: Do you mind if I ask if *you're* married?

David: I was counting on it. I am not married—true or false?

Joan: True. Yet there's something about you that says: a married man.

David: Divorced, twenty years ago. My wife left me to run away with a jockey. *(Removes the glasses.)* Possibly you noticed that my eyes are flecked with horse manure.

Joan: You have nice eyes. Any children?

David: A son. Whom I haven't seen since his mother moved to Melbourne to be closer to the stable.

Joan: That's a shame.

David: Au contraire. *(We are in the French-speaking part of Switzerland.)* Au contraire. My wife's leaving me was the first step of my deliverance from the need for human society. You are looking at the major triumph of mind over gregarious matter— the swinging hermit. More hot chocolate?

Joan: There isn't any more.

David: I know.

Joan: A hermit . . . but how do you get along without people?

David: Splendidly. Do you mind if I ski?

CUT TO:

David on skis, holding ski poles and executing fancy manoeuvres against the film background of a skier's-eye view of the spectacular descent on powder snow.

SOUND: *The rasp and swoosh of the ski run.*

CUT WITH:
David completing his run. Joan moves into the SHOT, *as he parks his shades on his head.*

David: Beautiful. Absolutely perfect conditions. Well! I guess this is where we do the toothpaste commercial.

Joan: The what?

David: You know—I tumble you into a snowdrift and we fool around flashing our teeth at each other, to show we use sexy toothpaste.

Joan: I don't use sexy toothpaste.

David: Whap, there goes our sponsor. Stand by for a public service message.

Joan: You're crazy.

David: This message was brought to you by your Mental Health Association. And remember: if you are driving somebody out of his mind—*drive defensively.*

Joan: You can't really believe that this is as much fun as getting out in the real snow, breathing the fresh air——

David: Ah-ha! Inhale!

Joan: What?

David: Inhale, inhale. Now, the air in your lungs is at least twenty per cent more pure than the air you would breathe on Mont Blanc—whose snow, by the way, is tattletale grey with fallout from Europe's booming industries. This air is filtered, humidified, de-humidified, by the sweetest name in breathing: Honeywell. Oh, Honeywell, Honeywell, thou hast my heart because thou givest me my lungs.

Joan: Okay, so the air is pure. It's still not . . . not the real thing.

David: *(Sobered)* It's true. There's almost no chance that I'll break my leg. *(During the following he turns off the* MUSIC *and removes his ski gear.)* This is *not* the real thing. For example— listen! What do you hear?

Joan: . . . Nothing.

David: Positively controlled silence. This Swiss *auberge* is sound-repellent. Quiet. Not the real thing. No voices of little children yelling obscenities at one another. No transistor radios whose rock stations are locked in mortal combat . . . *(He punches in radio rock.)* Not the real thing!

CUT TO:

David spraying an aerosol can.
   No smell of somebody else's suntan lotion, subtly blended with the onions frying on the hibachi upwind. Not the real thing!

CUT TO:

A shower of beer-can pulltabs, falling on Joan.
   You have just walked into a blizzard of beer-can pulltabs. But still—not the real thing!

He punches out the rock music. For a moment David and Joan stare at one another. He has drawn first blood in the battle he senses he shouldn't have started.

Joan: . . . It's not all like that.

David: What isn't?

Joan: The real Switzerland. The real world.

David: How do you know? Have you been there?

Joan: Not to Switzerland, yet, but I hope to go——

David: I have. I've been everywhere.

Joan: Everywhere?

David: Everywhere. No, not wealthy. I once worked as a newspaper columnist. Free flights, courtesy the airlines, to every exotic corner of the globe. From the fabled bazaars of the Marrakesh Hilton to Bora Bora's lagoons gobbed with tar—I wrote and raved about them all, except one or two unspoiled places that I kept to myself, secret. Then they too got discovered. Coca-colonization of the planet is now complete. Foreign places have nothing to offer you that you can't obtain much more comfortably in a rented can of travelogue.

Joan: I was hoping *I* might have something to offer *them.*

David: Ah. Well, in Baghdad they can use somebody who is really good at cleaning the sand out of the carburetors of Cadillacs.

Joan: I mean, offer to *people.* I *like* people.

David: Of course you do. And that's why ninety per cent of people travel: to meet other people. They're trying to get away from the people at home who know them for what they are, and go some place where people will see them as what they'd like to be. Do you know that there are rich old ladies who cruise round and round the world on P. & O. liners, and they never get off the ship? Suva, Colombo, Bombay, Vancouver—all these glamorous places—and what interests them is the people who embark. People travel to *escape*, dear girl, to escape themselves. Why else would they choose to be imprisoned, shut up, in the modern version of the iron maiden—a charter flight? Terrified . . . spilling hot coffee down their front . . . and hopelessly deluded that the jet aircraft can fly faster than the shadow of their life.

Joan: Maybe a person has to suffer in order to grow.

David: *(Fazed)* What?

Joan: I travelled across Canada one summer, with some other kids, in an old vw bus, all the way to Toronto. We had some rough miles, but I think I came back a better person.

David: I believe you're right. Young people *should* travel, preferably to Toronto, because it helps to build character. Getting there is half the agony, the other half provided by the Toronto Visitors Bureau. But me, my character is built. Of fully suffered brick. Landscaping by Father Time and Co.

Joan: Nobody should stop growing.

David: Why not? Who wants to have a high-rise character?

Joan: I do. Rising all the way to Heaven. What a lovely old roll-top desk. Is it an antique?

David: No, it's my office.

Joan: Oh. You work at home.

David: As could most people, in this day of telecommunication. People go to the office for the same reason that they travel: to get away from their wives, from their husbands, from their children, from themselves. The rush-hour traffic is the index of how desperate a man can become to avoid being trapped with his loved ones.

Joan: May I ask what kind of work you do?

David: I have my own public relations firm. I know what you're thinking: isn't it difficult to be in public relations when you are a hermit?

Joan: Well, isn't it?

David: It's impossible. That's what I like about it: the challenge. I specialize in *low-key* public relations. Clients that want to maintain a low, low profile.

Joan: Do you have many clients?

David: One. A chain of funeral homes. Hence the casket. A 1972 Sleeping Beauty. They had to recall all of this model, because of faulty handles. A person could be killed. *(During this David has taken off the Swiss garb, cloaking removal of the shorts under a voluminous caftan that he takes from the casket.)* I also do some free-lance writing—to keep body and soul together. May I ask what *you* do, when you're not crusading?

Joan: Nothing much, right now. I'm living at home. Sometimes I help my mother at the shop. She's a florist.

David: Ah, I knew we had something in common—floral offerings. *(He has primed the record player with French songs—Mireille Matthieu. It plays.)*

Joan: Well, I'd better be going.

David: That's right.

Joan: I'll leave you these copies of *Signpost*. No charge. *(Seated at the roll-top desk, she writes.)*

David: You're kind.

Joan: I'll write my name and phone number on the cover, in case you change your mind.

David: *(Standing beside the roll-top desk)* About what?

Joan: About being a hermit. It would be marvellous if you could come to our assembly. There will be sixty thousand people at the stadium, eating together, singing together, having a wonderful time.

David: Please. You're tainting my après-ski.

Joan: No, really. I'd like you to come.

David: I'm sure you would. It would mean another gold star on your report.

Joan: What do you mean?

David: I know how you people operate. *You* escape by means of conversion. You are preparing for launch to Jehovah's Kingdom, and I'm part of the rocket gantry. No relation to Elmer Gantry.

Joan: No. I wanted you to come for *your* sake. Right now I'm not thinking of escape to Jehovah's Kingdom. I'll settle for the hallway.

David: Done!

He slaps shut the cover of the roll-top desk at the same instant that she reaches into the desk to retrieve the magazines. CU David's face during:

Joan: Oh!

David: I've done it again.
MUSIC: *Out.*

END OF ACT ONE

ACT TWO

SCENE 5: INTERNAL SEQUENCE. INSIDE DAVID'S APART-MENT.

David pours another tray of ice cubes into the oven mitt. Joan is hatted and coated.

Joan: You needn't have called a cab for me. I'm used to——

David: Can't have you walking home in the dark. The West End teems with muggers.

Joan: *(Holding her hand)* I know.

David: There. The good host always has plenty of ice on hand. *(He gently eases her hand into the mitt.)*

Joan: I'm being a bother.

David: Please. You must allow me this act of contrition. I was very rude to you a moment ago. Cynical. Cynicism is the one sin I have to guard against. It comes from knowing more than is bad for you.

Joan: Thank you. That feels good.

David: Lucky you dropped in during Switzerland Night. Geneva is the headquarters of the International Red Cross. I can offer you help without having to speak your language.

Joan: Who helps *you*?

David: Well, I'm not entirely alone here, you know. I have Sarah.

Joan: Sarah?

David: Sarah Goldfish.

Joan: Oh. Goldfish.

David: What's the matter? You anti-Semitic? *(To Sarah)* Actually Sarah is excellent company, aren't you, dear? Don't talk with your mouth open . . . Ah!

Joan: What?

David: I believe she's jealous of you.

Joan: Of me! With you?

David: Good heavens, no. She's liberated. She's jealous because she thinks you've got a big, handsome red snapper eating out of your hand. *(To Sarah)* Shame on you, Sarah. Your eyes are bigger than your grotto.

Joan: May I ask you a personal question?

David: Certainly. To me or Sarah?

Joan: You. What do *you* do about sex?

David: Ah!

CUT TO:

David turning on projector. On screen, a stag film—a stripper, or belly dancer, in action but not offensively so. With:
MUSIC: *To suit.*

David: What do I do about sex? I've given the matter a lot of thought. I've come to the conclusion that there isn't much *anyone* can do about it.

Joan: Is that the best you can do?

David: What?

Joan: Stag movies. Why not a *real* woman?

CUT TO:

David beside projector, having turned it off.
MUSIC: *Out abruptly.*

David: A real woman. I tried one once. It didn't agree with me.

Joan: So you gave up.

David: There's an old saying: If at first you don't succeed, perhaps you should quit before you make a *real* fool of yourself.

Joan: That's a pity. There are some things that a man can't do for himself.

David: True. That is why I subscribe to the Bachelor Maid Agency.

Once a week an attractive girl comes to the flat and provides a complete service . . . provided I do the housecleaning.

Joan: I didn't mean that kind of sex. I meant love. Sex without love is like the sun without a sky.

David: Where did you read that?

Joan: In *Signpost*. It has a lot of good things.

David: I dispute the simile. Love is a means of obtaining property, in the person of another human being, and sex is the instrument of acquisition. As we all know, marriage is merely an expensive form of prostitution: not your money but your life. The only truly honest sex is that of a deep and meaningful sharing of pure lust.

Joan: You are wrong.

David: My dear, the only advantage in being considerably older than you is that I can claim more experience in this matter.

Joan: I doubt that. For two years I was a prostitute.

David: No.

Joan: Yes. At seventeen. I was deep into drugs, and I sold myself to get the money to pay for them. I know all there is to know about the expertise of sex. I have also met any number of men like you, as customers—emotional cowards, afraid to expose their tender feelings to a woman for fear of being hurt. It was like they'd undergone a vasectomy of the soul.

David: You read that in *Signpost*?

Joan: No. I *do* have some ideas of my own.

David: I concede the point. You are better qualified than I am to confirm that there is no such thing as unconditional sex . . . for a woman.

Joan: No? Suppose I were to offer myself to you now.

David: You mean, simulated sex?

Joan: I've never simulated sex.

David: Well! I guess that makes you a simulated virgin. What are you doing?

CUT TO:

Joan turning on the stereo, which resumes with the raunchy music. She is suddenly sensual, provocative—the stripper. She drops the oven mitt for openers.

MUSIC: *Reprise.*

David: You're just trying to confuse me.

Joan: Am I?

David: I know why you're doing this.

She sheds the hat and the coat.

Joan: Why?

David: Because a woman will do anything to win an argument.

Joan: Wrong. I am doing this as an act of charity.

David: Charity?

Joan: The good Christian gives alms to the man who hungers for food. Why not to the man who hungers for sex? They are both natural appetites.

David: You want to wrap your lovin' alms around me?

Joan: *(Unbuttoning)* Right.

CUT TO:

David turning off the stereo.

MUSIC: *Out.*

David: No. I don't accept charity.

Joan: Why not?

David: Because I have my pride! *I* want to feel needed too. You can button up your baksheesh.

Joan: You don't think I need you.

David: I do not.

Joan: Why?

David: Because of an unfortunate combination of circumstances: I am over forty but I don't look like Paul Newman.

Joan: Perhaps I don't want Paul Newman.

David: Don't play games with me, young lady. Every woman wants Paul Newman, except the younger ones, who want Alice Cooper. You want tall blue eyes and the promise of violence.

Joan: Tall blue eyes?

David: You know what I mean. I repeat: don't try to play games with me. It's like asking Bobby Fischer for a game of checkers.

Joan: Why must it be a game? Why can't sex be an expression of love, not possessive love, but love as sharing a beautiful experience?

David: . . . Zo.

CUT TO:

David, wearing absurdly thick glasses, and putting on a frock coat, taken from the casket.

MUSIC: *The burbly, bland piped music of the Lobby Scene.*

David: *(German accent)* You wish an analysis of love. *(Waving her to the casket as couch)* Ve just haf time before the taxicab comes.

CUT TO:

David seated in swivel chair. Joan lies on the casket.

David: *(Consulting notepad)* Love. I have made a thorough study of love as a human requirement. Primarily, it is a means of self-identification.

Joan: You have nice eyes.

David: The average human being needs company as a crutch for the ego. As Sartre said: "We find ourselves in the eyes of others." Even a dog or a cat, as a pet, is sustenance to our awareness of being somebody: the master of the loving one. When a pet dies, the owner feels diminished, because he has lost the mirror of himself as a lovable being.

Joan: You're a pussycat.

David: This is why I keep only a goldfish. Goldfish do not live long, and they show a minimum of affection for anything but another goldfish.

Joan: Did anyone ever tell you you look like Paul Newman?

David: What we usually call love is the feeling we have for someone we consider to be superior to ourselves—physically, intellectually. If that person pays some attention to us, we are overwhelmed by the evidence that we are worth more than we thought we were. In short, we are in love.

Joan: Oh, David! We are, aren't we?

David: The more proof we have of our personal worth, the less need we have for love from other individuals. Glamorous film stars, adulated by the public, can survive for years without love, whereas love is needed desperately by small children, homely women, and middle-aged men whose wives have run away with a jockey.

Joan: Then you *do* need love.

David: Nein. I recognize love for what it is—an ego trip. Another form of travel. Another kind of escape.

Joan: Okay! What's wrong with escape? If you're in jail, why not escape?

David: *(Dropping accent)* I am not in jail! I——

Joan: You *are*! Look at all the locks on your door. Look at your no windows. You're in solitary confinement! You've put yourself in the hole.

David: Wrong! Out *there* is the penitentiary. Pascal said: "All of man's unhappiness comes from his inability to remain alone in a room." I——

Joan: To hell with Pascal!

David: To hell with Pascal? Pascal was the greatest religious philosopher of—

Joan: I don't care! He was sick. What's the good of not being unhappy if you can't be happy?

David: . . . Would you mind repeating the question?

Joan: What's the good of not being unhappy if you can't be happy? Sure, out there you fall in love, you get hurt, you laugh, you cry. . . . That's what life is all about.

David: If that's what life is all about, I'm not living!

Joan: I agree!

David: Because it is *vulgar*! It is also woman. Your sex loves turbulence, people, things happening. Turmoil! In the whole history of mankind there has never been a successful female hermit!

Joan: Because we have more sense! *(She mounts the bike and starts pedalling.)* Look at this silly thing. You go no place. Why not pedal a *real* bike, through a field of sweet clover. . . .

David: Private property. Trespassers will be prosecuted.

Joan: . . . On a bicycle built for two. We'll have a picnic, in the tall blue grass. . . .

SOUND: *Downpour and wind.*

David sits in the rowing machine and rows.

David: Bad luck about the cloudburst. Lucky I have this life-raft—capacity, one person. . . .

MUSIC: *"Raindrops"*

Joan: I love biking in the rain. When we reach the summer cottage, we'll take off our wet things and sit together in front of the fire. . . .

David: A disaster. The flash flood has turned the whole valley into a lake. I'm the sole survivor. . . .

Joan gets off the bike and moves towards David.

Joan: No, there's another.

David: You're walking on water!

Joan: The power of love.

David: You're cheating!

Joan: You're right. *(She collapses into his arms.)* I've almost drowned. Help me.

David: Help you? Help you how?

Joan: Mouth-to-mouth resuscitation.

David: I don't know how to give mouth-to-mouth resuscitation.

Joan: I'll teach you.

SOUND: *A banging on the door.*

David: Thank God! It's your cab.

MUSIC: *Out.*

SOUND: *Out.*

CUT TO:

David opening the door with frantic eagerness. The person who has knocked is a young man—Robbie—good-looking in a lean and hungry way. He wears a black leather jacket.

David: Come in! Come in! *(Removes glasses.)*

Robbie enters. He is out of puff, sweating, nervous. A very insecure young thug.

David: *(Indicating Joan)* There's your fare. You *are* the cab driver? *(Robbie kicks the door shut behind him, bolts it, and produces a wicked-looking switchblade.)*

You're not the cab driver.

Robbie: Don't try to answer this door.

David: *Now* he tells me!

CUT TO:

END OF ACT TWO

ACT THREE

SCENE 6: INTERNAL SEQUENCE. INSIDE DAVID'S APART-
MENT.

Robbie: *(Menacing Joan and David with knife)* Do what I say, and
   nobody gets cut.

Joan: You're a fugitive. The police are after you.

Robbie: Head of the class, baby. You can sit right over there . . .
   teacher's pet.

Joan sits on one of the café chairs.

David: What did you do?

Robbie: I carved up a middle-aged freak who asked too many
   questions. In the other chair. *(David sits in the other chair. Robbie
   listens at the door.)* Marvy. Now, just dummy up. Like, nobody
   home, right? Nobody here but us creeps.

Joan: Who are you calling "creeps"?

Robbie: *(Gesturing at the equipment)* You got everything here but
   the massage table. *(He moves to the door to the balcony.)*

David: Now see here——

Robbie: Shuddup! . . . Remember?

David: There's no need to shut up. This room is sound-resistant.
   Not entirely soundproof, but ninety-two per cent . . .

Robbie: Yeah? *(He opens the double, baffled door to the balcony.)*

SOUND: *Police siren from street below.*

Robbie takes a peek at the action in the street, then closes the door.

SOUND: *Out.*

Robbie: Hey, man, it *is* soundproof. I come to the right place. *(Sits
   in swivel chair.)* Don't mind me. Go ahead with whatever you
   were doing.

*(Joan and David look at the rowing machine and at each other,
discomfited.)*

   Go ahead. Don't be shy. I don't shock easy.

David: The young lady and I were discussing means of escape.

Robbie: From what?

David: From reality.

Robbie: Yeah? Who won?

Joan: Who won what?

Robbie: The argument.

David: I did.

Joan: You did not!

David: I did. See what happens when you open your door to the world? In walks violence.

Robbie: Who are you calling violent?

David: Well, aren't you?

Robbie: You call me violent, and I'll slit your throat. *(Laughs.)* That's kinda funny, don't you think?

David: Hilarious.

Robbie: *(Savouring it)* You call me violent, and I'll slit your throat.

Joan: *(Smiling)* I thought it was funny.

Robbie: Yeah?

David: She's trying to get you on her side.

Robbie: And what's wrong with that?

David: Do you know what she is? She's a member of Crusaders for Christ.

Robbie: *(Staring at Joan, disillusioned)* You're not a hooker?

Joan: Not any more. I found a better way of meeting people.

David: Why don't you ask *him* if he has a room to spare?

Joan: All right, I will. *(To Robbie)* The Crusaders are having their convention here in the city. Would you have a spare room you could rent?

Robbie: You're putting me on.

Joan: No, I'm not. Let me show you the latest issue of *Signpost* . . .

Robbie: Stay right where you are. *(To David)* If she's a Crusader, how come she's in your room fooling around?

David: I pinched her fingers.

Robbie: *(To Joan)* That what turns you on?

David: I pinched her fingers in the *door*. I asked her in to try to administer first aid.

Robbie: And now you're administering first aid to me. You're a regular little St. John's Ambulance, aren't you?

David: No. I don't want to seem inhospitable, but how long do you intend to stay here? I mean, roughly—hours, days, weeks . . . ?

Robbie: I'll be here till I go.

David: Good. Just so long as I can plan . . .

Robbie: Okay, man—cut the smart-ass. I'm telling you right now . . . I don't like your face.

David: Neither do I.

Joan: *I* like your face. Except for one thing. I hope you don't mind me asking a personal question . . .

Robbie: He don't mind.

Joan: . . . but, why do you always have that smile on your face?

David: *(Smiling)* What smile?

Joan: *That* smile. Your mouth is sort of . . . warped.

David looks at Robbie, who nods and flashes a tin smile.

David: Oh, that. I don't call that a smile. I put on a happy face, in public. Doesn't everybody?

Joan: I don't.

Robbie: Me neither. Show me a smiler, and I'll show you a loser.

David: I'm not a loser.

Robbie: You're a loser. Like them other losers . . . your smiling high-school principal, your minister smiling at the half-empty church. Like that dame smiling in the picture . . .

David: . . . The *Mona* Loser?

Joan: I think smiling like that is a defence mechanism. You smile so people won't know how you *really* feel. I used to do it all the time, when I was on the street.

David: I *beg* your pardon?

Joan: *(To Robbie)* The same way you're smiling now.

The smile vanishes from Robbie's face.

Robbie: Shut up. Both of you. We're gonna have two minutes of silence, out of respect for my nerves.

For about ten seconds, all three sit silent.

Robbie: *(At David)* And wipe that smile off your face!

The smile vanishes from David's face.

Joan: Oh, I like you much better that way.

Robbie: *(Menacing David)* How about if I make him cry? *(To David)* You'll be irresistible.

Joan: Oh, don't be such a bully. I've seen lots of your kind, on Davie Street. I bet I can even guess why the cops are after you. Some tinhorn attempt at robbery. A bank? No, too dangerous. Not even a service station. A Chinese greengrocer! You tried to hold up a Chinese greengrocer, and he pulled a stalk of rhubarb on you.

Robbie: Baby, you are asking for it.

Joan: You don't frighten me. In me is the righteousness of God's kingdom, in which all crime shall be cleansed from the earth. Including scum like you.

Robbie swings back his arm to backhand-slap her face, but freezes at:

SOUND: *Pounding on the door.*

Joan: Come in!

Robbie: Why you . . .

David: Don't touch her!

SOUND: *Pounding on door.*

All three stare at the door. CU of doorknob turning. It stops.

Robbie: They've gone. *(To David)* You still want to be a hero?

David: No. I'm only brave on impulse. Given time to consider a situation, I usually manage to conform to the contemporary image of the anti-hero.

Joan: I don't believe it. For a moment there you became *involved.* I'm glad it happened. . . .

David: I did *not* become involved!

Joan: . . . You *are* a human being, after all.

David: I am *not* a human being!

David stares at Robbie.

Robbie: You don't get no argument from me.

David: *(To Joan)* Not what *you* mean by a human being. You——

Robbie: Shut up. *(To Joan)* As I was about to say, before we were interrupted, it wasn't no Chinese greengrocer we hit. It was an appliance store. A *major* appliance store.

Joan: What happened?

Robbie: My partner musta tripped a burglar alarm. We drew a crowd . . . all wearing blue. But, so the evening won't be a total loss . . . let's have *your* cash. All of it.

Joan: The only money I have is what I've collected selling copies of the Crusaders' magazines.

Robbie: I'm not proud. Let's have it.

David: You'd steal money from a religious organization?

Robbie: Sure. It's deductible. *(Laughs.)* It's deductible.

David: *(To Joan)* Another nice thing about Switzerland . . . the echo.

Robbie: What?

David: Before you joined us, St. Joan and I were discussing Switzerland. I have exactly six dollars on the premises. In my wallet. In the bedroom. On the night table.

Robbie: Get it. *(David goes to fetch the wallet.)* Bring the whole wallet. I love looking at photos of the kids.

Joan: *(Sotto)* That was an unkind thing to say. David is divorced.

Robbie: So he's divorced. He's been taking cheap shots at *me*. I don't remember hearing you complain.

Joan: You're younger than he is.

David arrives back in time to overhear this.

David: *(Tossing the wallet to Robbie)* I made a mistake. There's only five dollars. *(At Joan)* I blew a buck on a bottle of Geritol.

Robbie: Sit down.

David: You're sure I'm not keeping you?

Robbie: Positive, Pops.

Joan: Why do you have to steal people's money? If you need cash, you can go on welfare.

Robbie: I got expensive tastes, baby.

Joan: Drugs. *(Robbie smiles at her.)* Let me guess. Coke? Heroin? Acid?

Robbie: Coke, heroin, acid . . . whadya take me for, some high-school kid?

Joan: What then?

Robbie: . . . Would you believe . . . liquor?

David and Joan look at one another.

David: Booze. The escape route of our fathers.

Joan: *(To Robbie)* But surely you don't need to resort to crime to pay for your habit, when it's alcohol.

Robbie: I happen to like the imported stuff.

David: Old World charm, without the nuisance of learning the language. I remember that the most memorable moment of my last trip to Europe was standing in the duty-free shop of Orly airport and buying a bottle of Courvoisier brandy for five dollars less than it would have cost me in Canada. A truly moving cultural experience. *(To Robbie)* May I offer you a drink?

Robbie: I don't drink when I'm working.

David: Oh. Sorry. Thought you were finished. *(Pause.)* I have a rather rare Bavarian beer——

Joan: Don't encourage him!

David: I beg your pardon?

Joan: If he doesn't want to drink, leave him alone.

David: Good Lord. You're not only a Crusader, you're a *dry* Crusader.

Joan: I certainly am.

David: Your father was an alcoholic.

Joan: My father was *not* an alcoholic! . . . My *mother* was an alcoholic.

David: There is such a thing as *civilized* drinking. Isn't it possible that . . . *(To Robbie)* May we have your name?

Robbie: No.

Joan: I call him "Robbie". *(To Robbie)* You don't mind?

David: Isn't it possible that Robbie is a civilized drinker? *(To Robbie)* What is your favourite drink?

Robbie: A double Scotch, with two bennies.

David: Oh. *(To Joan)* The trouble with you fundamentalists is that you are intolerant of other people's means of escaping reality. Honour thy neighbour's cop-out!

Joan: I will *not* honour my neighbour's cop-out! You don't know what my father went through, living with a woman who couldn't get out of bed in the morning without her slug of gin.

Robbie: Maybe I will have that drink after all.

David: Good. *(He goes to the fridge and takes out a bottle of Bavarian beer.)* I was going to have it myself this evening, with my Swiss Gruyère. *(To Joan)* I'd offer you a drink. But I'm out of goat's milk.

Joan: I'm not thirsty.

Robbie: *(To David)* Hold it. Throw me the bottle . . . underhand.
David tosses Robbie the bottle.

David: Please don't open it with your teeth. It can . . . *(Robbie knocks off the bottle lid on the edge of the roll-top desk.)* . . . damage the enamel.
Robbie, having extracted the bills from the wallet, throws the wallet to David.

Robbie: Keep the change.

David: Thank you. Is it all right if we have a little music? It helps to cover the lulls in the conversation.

Robbie: *What* lulls? We haven't had one decent lull since I come in here.
David turns on the stereo.
MUSIC: Sound of Music.
David turns on the projector—The Swiss Chalet, a still. During the following, he takes a bottle of French wine, already opened, from the kitchen counter and pours himself a glass.

David: Two people can be silent together. Three people have to keep talking. That's why I was so glad to give up cocktail parties forever, because if you stop talking the hostess gives you a look that turns you into an anchovy. *(Raising glass)* A French Burgundy, but close enough.

Robbie: So you got this set-up. Sorry, man, but you overdone it.

David: Overdone what?

Robbie: Avoidin' crowds. They're gonna come for you . . . with a butterfly net.

David: You may be right. But let me try to convince you. After all, we have a lot in common. We're both antisocial. But you express your rejection of society in a way that is, if you don't mind my saying so, conventional. In fact, old-fashioned.

Robbie: Whadya mean, old-fashioned?

David: Robbery. Violence. You're *fighting* society, as outlaws have done for thousands of years. And usually lost. Instead of trying to destroy *their* world, why not use their technology to create your *own* world, within your own four walls?

Joan: Your four walls won't spare you from the day of judgment.

David: Oh, but they will! The day of judgment has been moved forward. The world is rapidly running out of energy. What will all those frantically mobile millions do when gasoline costs fifty dollars a gallon . . . if they can find it?

Robbie: Steal it.

David: Won't you be a little conspicuous, the only car on the road? No! The future belongs to the static. I am riding the motionless wave of the future. You are looking at the pioneer of The Stationary Movement. When others will be trying to find salvation in bicycle clips, I shall be the patriarch of staying put.

Robbie: No, thanks. I already been on the wave of the future: I did six months at Oakalla.

Joan: That's what *I* say.

Robbie: You did time at Oakalla?

Joan: Kingston. *(To David)* What you've pioneered is the do-it-yourself prison.

David: The locks are on *my* side of the door.

Joan: Locks will set you free?

David: *And* you!

Joan: Me? I don't even lock the bathroom.

David: Good Lord.

Robbie: Me neither. *I* leave the door open when I'm in the can. Which is as close as I'll get to The Stationary Movement. *(Laughs.)* The Stationary Movement.

Joan: Me too. I've got to be going. *(She gets up and starts to put on her coat.)*

Robbie: Hold it. I'll tell you when you can go.

Joan: I have to go *now*. I was assigned this whole block to canvass this evening, and that is what I am going to do.

Robbie: Don't push me, baby.

Joan: Look, if it's my calling the police you're scared of, I won't. I swear.

David: She swears. From her, that's an oath with clout.

Robbie: Uh-uh. I don't trust nobody. You stay.

Joan: Then I shall have to hit you. *(She picks up the oven mitt.)*

Robbie: *(Grinning)* Gee, she's gonna hit me. *(He makes no effort to defend himself against the blow from the oven mitt, and its load of ice cubes, that Joan delivers to the side of his head.)*

SOUND: *Whump.*

Robbie is dazed. Joan kicks the knife out of his hand. David picks it up. Robbie clutches his wrist.

Robbie: Ow! You broke my wrist.

Joan: I think you'll find that it's only sprained. *(To David)* I once took a course in karate at the YW.

David: They do good work.

Robbie: What was in that oven mitt?

David: Ice cubes. Medicinal.

Joan: Let me see your wrist.

Robbie: Stay away from me!

Joan: I want to help you.

Robbie: You gotta canvass the whole block, remember?

Joan: Shut up and let me see your wrist.

Joan examines the wrist during:

David: Better let her look at your wrist or she'll break your leg.

Joan: *(Putting the oven mitt on Robbie's hand.)* It's just a sprain. This will help to keep down the swelling.

David: Sorry I don't have more ice cubes. I didn't know it would be a large party . . .

Robbie: I can take that knife away from you, even with a bad wrist.

David: I'm sure you can, but I shall almost certainly cut myself and bleed all over you. Will it help you to leave the building unnoticed . . . covered with blood and wearing an oven mitt?

SOUND: *The telephone, on the roll-top desk, rings.*

Good Lord. It never rings when I'm alone.

Joan: Well, answer it.

David: It's either the police or my mother.

Robbie: Don't answer it.

David: *(To Robbie)* You'd better hope it's the police.

END OF ACT THREE

ACT FOUR

SCENE 7: INTERNAL SEQUENCE. INSIDE DAVID'S APART-MENT.

David: *(Picks up the phone receiver.)* . . . Yes, Mr. Simmons. . . . Seen anyone suspicious in the building? Only the regular tenants. . . . I see. . . . Yes, thank you, Mr. Simmons. *(Hangs up.)* The building superintendent. The police are still watching the lobby.

Joan: You didn't tell him about Robbie.

David: No, I didn't.

Robbie: How come?

David: I don't know. It just . . . didn't seem to be any of my business. . . . Isn't my evening in Switzerland ruined enough without having a lot of cops tramping all over my Alps?

Joan: I knew it! You *are* a human being. You relate to other people. You can't help it.

David: Oh, yes I can. How *dare* you assume that I should relate to other people! You and your damn brotherhood! It's easy for *you* to be brotherly . . . you're a woman!

Robbie: Cops still in the lobby, huh?

Joan: What has my being a woman got to do with it?

David: A woman is a primitive! She loves to suffer. She cries. She laughs. She *survives*. I'm a man, and I can anticipate all the trouble I'm getting myself into. It offends my intelligence to invite suffering that I should be able to avoid!

Joan: *Nobody* can avoid suffering!

Robbie: Did he say how many cops were in the lobby?

David: No. *(To Joan)* Do you think your Jehovah suffers? Hell, no. Because He has sense enough to stay clear of creation. God is my kind of shut-in!

Joan: You dare to compare yourself to God, this freaky little flat to the throne of Heaven?

Robbie: That reminds me . . . can I use the john?

David throws him the wallet.

David: First, my five dollars back.

Robbie puts the bills back into the wallet, drops it, and goes to the bathroom during:

(*To Joan*) What's wrong with living like God? *He* isn't interested in the games people play, and neither am I. I don't know about Him, but *I* prefer talking to myself because there's always the chance I'll say something I haven't heard before.

Joan: Of all the . . . colossal ego!

David: Who . . . me or God?

Joan: You! God doesn't need help. One day you will. You'll be sick. You'll be old. Who will you talk to then? Who will talk to *you*?

David: Ah-ha! The notorious death scene of the loner!

SOUND: *Off, toilet flushing.*

It's true, he *does* leave the door open. (*To Joan*) You think I haven't anticipated the end, with nobody to wave bye-bye?

During this and the following, David changes the cassette on the projector—film of interior of hospital, a patient's-eye view, terminating in the semi-private ward. He also changes the cassette on the stereo.

MUSIC: *The bland piped music.*

David: Would you care to join me in a death scene?

CUT TO:

David, in white robe, lying in the casket, covered by white sheet. His hair too is white.

The last escape. The lucky ones find the quick exit . . . a heart attack. Others, we who thought more than was good for us, God punishes with the longer route of cancer. Ah, Nursie!

(*Joan comes to his bedside. She wears a nurse's uniform and carries a tray on which are cans of film and cassettes of recorded music.*)

You've brought my sedation. No get-well cards. It's a blessing not to have friends, at a time like this. The poor devils would be going out of their minds trying to find a get-well card for somebody with a terminal disease. Somebody who knows, and who knows they know. The greeting-card industry has never come to grips with reality. That's why it makes so much money.

Joan sets the tray on the table.

Joan: The doctor has ordered "No Visitors".

David: Just like the medical profession, to take the credit. There are no visitors because that's the way I arranged my life. No buzzards to perch on my cot, to audition the last gasp. To bring me bouquets of lies about how much better I look today, and ask when is the hospital going to kick me out of this bed and give it to somebody who is *really* sick. Visitors . . . in the name of former neglect, past sins, or the last will and testament. Take down the "No Visitors" sign, Nursie . . . it's painting the lily. *(Laughs like Robbie.)* Painting the lily.

Joan: Okay. But don't forget *I'm* here. *(She goes towards the door.)*

David: How could I forget? It's for you that I am being bright and brave. A little soldier, Nursie. When you're at the nursing station, talking to the other nurses, I want you to say . . . what's my room number?

CUT TO:

Joan, who opens door to hall to read the number.

Joan: Eight twelve. *(As she is about to shut it, Robbie's arm obstructs her. Their dialogue is over David's tirade in the background.)* You're back.

Robbie: They're still redecorating the lobby . . . blue. *(Shuts door behind them.)* What games you playing now?

Joan: He's dying. I'm Nursie.

Robbie: Yeah? Is this a private fantasy, or can anybody get in?

David: *(Eyes closed)* I want you to say: "He's a little soldier, eight twelve. You'd swear he was going home tomorrow morning." And the other nurses say: "He's so uncomplaining. Yesterday I forgot to empty his bedpan. Did he complain? No, sir. He just asked if he could borrow a cork. . . ."

On Joan's appraising look at Robbie

CUT TO:

David: I want you to tell the other nurses that I'm the best patient you ever had . . . including the football player.

Joan takes his wrist to check his pulse.

Joan: That's exactly what I say to the other nurses.

David: You're lying. You've seen 'em all, haven't you? The drags. The cheerios. You see behind all the false fronts . . . right? You see right inside, to the sheer terror that is the little soldier's standard equipment. What you'd really appreciate from me is a positive silence. You have a date with your boyfriend, and having to argle-bargle with eight one two distracts you from the pleasure of looking forward to his embrace.

Joan: I don't have a boyfriend. Not one with that kind of embrace.

David stares at Joan, who continues to hold his hand.

David: . . . No. You shouldn't have told me that. Don't you see, you are the impartial witness to my dying. I have planned to enjoy one of life's last little ironies: that we spend our lives with a variety of people, but we meet death in the company of strangers . . . the patient in the next bed . . . the house doctor . . . the nurse. See, you have to wear your name on a little tag. We're attending a convention, the convention of . . . passing on. Just because I have invited you to my room is no reason to become sincere.

Joan: *Please* stop smiling.

David: Sorry. *Risus sardonicus.* Rushing it a bit. *(Stops smiling. Stares straight ahead.)*

Slowly, deliberately, Joan lifts the hand she holds to her lips, and kisses it.

David: *(Still staring)* What are you doing?

Joan: I kissed your hand.

David: That isn't on my list of medication. Just because you wash my private parts doesn't give you the right to kiss my hand.

Joan: I kissed your hand because I feel sorry for you. For your being so alone.

David: No, you don't. You feel sorry for yourself. You look at me, poised to hop the twig, and you say to yourself: "There I'll be, one day. If I don't feel sorry for him, why should anyone feel sorry for me?" Just like a funeral—and here I know whereof I spook—the funeral that is held not for the dead but for the living. Have you ever watched the crowd coming out of the chapel service at a funeral home? As merry a bunch as you'll see, outside of a Charlie Chaplin film festival.

Joan: Oh, how you twist everything! You make it sound as though there is no such thing as an unselfish act.

David: Right on! The Golden Rule says it all: "Do unto others as you would have them do unto you" . . . the operative word being *you.* Selfish! Selfish!

Joan: All right! So we're selfish! What does it matter, so long as

what we do is *good* for another person? Like . . . rescuing a total
stranger from a fire.

David: Too late, Nursie. If there's a Hell, I'm for it.

Joan: Why?

David: God doesn't want me up there. I know too much. Only nice,
gregarious people like you who believe in altruism go to Heaven.
Smart-asses are fed to the furnace. Draw the curtain, Nursie. The
comedy is over.

Joan: No, it isn't.

David: What?

Joan: You *do* have a visitor.

David: *(As Joan goes to the door)* What do you mean? No visitors
are allowed at the death-bed except members of the immediate
family.

Joan: *(At the door)* This is a member of the immediate family. *(To
the unseen visitor)* You may come in now.

*Robbie enters. No oven mitt. He wears David's ski garb: sweater,
toque, and sunglasses.*

Robbie: Hi, Dad.

David: You? I thought you'd left.

Robbie: I came back. The elevator ain't working.

Joan: That's right. Some nut has been fooling with the emergency
button.

David: *(Sinking)* Some nut . . . who attacks rubber plants.

Robbie: How you feeling, Dad?

David: *(To Joan)* You put him up to this.

Joan: He wanted to participate. He's interested in group therapy.

David: No, thanks. I'm not having *this.*

Joan: You already had it. Twenty years ago. Your son.

David: You told him?

Robbie: *(Pushing sunglasses on top of head)* She didn't have to. I'd
know you any place . . . Daddy.

*Joan and Robbie sit on opposite sides of the bed, as David struggles
to get out of it.*

David: Get him out of here! I'm dying!

Robbie: You've changed, got older, but you're still the same basic creep that's to blame for Mom being an alcoholic.

David: I'm to blame? . . . You are *not* my son! *(To Joan)* He is not——

Joan: How do you know? You haven't seen him for years.

Robbie: You're him, no question. I may not be your son, but you're my old man. Dead inside.

David: Oh, no, you don't. You're not tagging *me* as representative of a generation of male parents. I didn't even *want* a child.

Robbie: *(To Joan)* Mom told me that's what he used to tell her. No wonder she ran away with a truck driver.

David: A jockey! It was a jockey!

Joan: Does it really matter what he was steering?

David: My God.

Joan: You see? You can't escape. You *are* a part of humanity.

David: I can! I just made an error: I didn't die fast enough. Aaargh. *(He falls back into the casket,* in extremis.*)*

Joan: What is it?

David: I am lapsing into my coma. And not a moment too soon.

Joan: No! You can't die.

David: Why not?

Joan: Because . . . it's chicken!

David stares at her for a moment, then:

David: *(Chicken)* . . . puck, puck, puuu-ck! *(Dies.)*

With one quick movement, Robbie flips shut the lid of the casket. He sits on it.

Joan: Oh!

Robbie: I thought he'd never go.

Joan: Open it! He'll suffocate.

Robbie: I want him to know how it feels. Don't you?

Joan: No! Revenge is sick. You've got to learn to forgive your parents, the way I did. Now——

The top, or viewing, half of the casket swings open and David pops up.

David: Get off my coffin!

Robbie: Sorry, Daddy-O. I didn't know it was your coffin. I thought it was a horizontal phone booth, and somebody up there called your number. *(Laughs.)* Somebody up there called your number.

David: *(Near tears)* It's not fair . . . it's not fair! I expected the unexpected, but this is ridiculous.

Joan: *(To Robbie)* Don't you think you'd better go?

Robbie: Yeah. I've paid my respects. *(He moves towards the door.)* Thanks, Dad, for the cover from the cops. Too bad you couldna done it twenty years ago. *(Opens door.)* See yuh, Nursie.

Joan: I hope so.

(Robbie checks the corridor, winks at Joan, and slips out, closing the door behind him.)

Do you want me to lock the door?

David: It . . . doesn't seem to matter any more.

David clambers out of the casket during:

Joan: It's my fault. Your evening is ruined. I'm sorry.

David: My evening? My whole way of life!

Joan: I *am* sorry. If——

David: Oh, you couldn't have done it alone, wreaked devastation on such a scale. *(Looking upward)* You had help. God has punished me for the sin of intellectual pride . . . hubris.

Joan: You really believe that?

David: As an agnostic I *can't* believe it. I can only suspect it very strongly.

Joan goes to the projector and turns off the hospital background. She then silences the tape of piped music and tunes the radio till she finds:

MUSIC: *For Lovers.*

David: What are you doing?

Joan: I want to make amends. *(She starts to unbutton.)*

David: Oh, no! Not again! You're taking advantage of my weakened condition!

Joan goes to him, takes his grey wig and tosses it away.

Joan: There. You look better already.

David: Joan, for*get* it! You didn't help me with my escape, why should I help you with yours?

Joan: Because you're a nice person.

David: Never!

CUT TO:

David lying in the bed in his real bedroom. He is seen bare from the waist up, half propped up on the pillow. His afterglow is slightly glazed.

MUSIC: *Out.*

David: The bedroom.

Joan is completing getting dressed in her own clothes.

Joan: Pardon?

David: This is where it happens. Where the baying hounds of reality catch us up. Conception, birth, illness, death . . . they cut off our escape right here, on this . . . absurd little plateau.

Joan goes to him and kisses his mouth, a gentle, tender kiss.

Joan: You were running the wrong way.

David: No. My mistake was to have a bedroom. I should have slept in there, in Fantasyland, in a hammock. I should have rented this room to your convention of Crusaders for Christ.

Joan: It's not too late. I'll put your name down.

She walks into the living room, watched by a flabbergasted David. Holding a sheet around him, he follows her into the other room, where Joan is picking up her satchel and clipboard.

David: Do you *always* canvass like this?

Joan: No. Sometimes I'm not invited in.

David: You're smug. You think you've scored a point for the God of love.

Joan: Well, haven't I?

David: No way! Nothing is changed! Nothing! We have both responded to a rudimentary urge to reproduce the species. Nothing more! My life style remains intact!

Joan: Maybe you're right.

David: Don't you maybe me! The flesh is weak. But my philosophy of the viable existence for a man standing on the brink of the twenty-first century . . . *that* is inviolate!

Joan: Maybe . . . Sorry. I hope that you and your philosophy will be very happy together, but I doubt it. Now I must be going.

David: Wait a minute! You think that you can . . . insinuate yourself into this cloister, and after you have satisfied your lust for salvation . . . walk out?

Joan: I thought you wanted to be alone.

David: I do! I want you to go! . . . but not till you tell me: why *me*?

Joan goes to him.

Joan: Because I had to find out.

David: Find out what?

Joan: What you are like. *Really* like.

David: What *am* I really like?

Joan: What I thought . . . gentle, and kind.

David: Thank you, but surely there was a less . . . personal way of finding that out. Whatever became of woman's intuition?

Joan: So much of you is make-believe, there is only one way for a woman to get to know the real you.

David: So! *That's* where the real me lurks, ready to blow the gaffe. Achilles was lucky . . . all he had to worry about was his heel. Lord Almighty. . . .

Joan kisses him lightly on the mouth.

Joan: Goodbye, David.

David: Wait! Wait a minute.

Joan: *(At the door)* Yes?

David: Uh . . . will you be making any more house calls, tonight?

Joan: *(Shaking her head)* I'm going home. I've had a very successful evening. Thank you.

David: You're welcome.

(Joan opens the door, goes out, and closes the door behind her. David stands staring at the door.)

It never happened. I'm the victim of wild hallucination. Somewhere amid the glories of the Alps I ate a bad yogurt.

(Automatically he goes to the door to secure the various locks and bolts. He recognizes the barn from which the horse has bolted, and abandons the procedure.)

The hell with it.

(For a moment he gazes about at the sullied apparatus of his private world. Then, with the misdirected bounce of the born loser:)

Okay! So Switzerland didn't turn out too good. Do we abandon the whole world of tomorrow because one country proved to be a bummer? We do not! You were right, Sarah! We should have spent the evening in Hawaii. But it's not too late. I think I have a can of Polynesia . . .

CUT TO:

David trying too hard to enjoy himself in a Hawaiian setting: He wears a vivid shirt and a lei of artificial flowers garnered from funeral wreaths, and he sits in the casket as converted into an outrigger canoe, including the sail. He wields a paddle, with excessive vigour, against the projected background of scenes of Waikiki Beach, Diamond Head, and mountainous surf.

MUSIC: *Stridently Hawaiian.*

David: This is the life, eh, Sarah? The mind swept clean by the fragrant Trade Winds of the Pacific! The long, green combers sweeping clean upon the coral beach, unpolluted by fat ladies from Peoria! A brisk paddle across the lagoon, out to the reef . . . don't worry, Sarah: these tropical fish are incredibly colourful but they have foul dispositions . . . then we glide serenely back to the little grass shack that Kaiser hasn't bought, for a cool, refreshing slice of paw-paw with lemon. . . . How does that grab you, Sarah?

MUSIC: *Dies in pain.*

Sarah?

The projected scene has turned upside down.

CUT TO:

Sarah floating belly up in her bowl.

David: No!

CUT TO:

David.

David: You can't do this to me! *Now . . . now . . .* of all the rotten, stinking tricks, you had to choose *now* to die. . . . You really hated me, didn't you? You hated me because living with you was as close as I could get to living alone. You waited . . . all these months . . . pretending to be happy . . . till now, when I'm vulnerable, then . . . poof, you take the easy way out. You . . . you . . . female!

CUT TO:

Sarah, unmoved, then to David sitting in the swivel chair at the roll-top desk, in his dressing gown, quill pen in hand, ready to enter the record of the evening's events in a black book. He does not look radiant.

David: Okay. So it was a bad day for the experiment. Banting must have had his bad days . . . Alexander Graham Bell . . . Dr. Frankenstein. There must have been days when Pascal had to leave the room.

(Having rallied his flagging resolve, he starts to write. The quill nib breaks. The last straw. He tosses the pen over his shoulder and closes the book. He then notices the copies of Signpost *that Joan left on the desk. He draws back, alarmed.)*

Condition red, condition red. Alien object from another world, possibly radioactive. Implement Disposal Plan A, for Adam. . . .

CUT TO:

David, wearing protective goggles, as he uses a pair of culinary forceps, plus oven mitts, to pick up the copies of Signpost *very gingerly and carry them to the wastebasket beside the desk.*
MUSIC: *Weird, electronic version of "Abide With Me".*
David successfully transfers the first copy of the magazine to the wastebasket, but with the other issue, the one with Joan's name and phone number on the cover, as he withdraws the forceps from the wastebasket they tear off that part of the cover that is most toxic. He shakes the forceps, trying to dislodge the deadly scrap of paper. It adheres, magnetically, with preternatural insistence. At last he has to pick the paper off the forceps with his mitt. He discards the forceps and tries to drop that paper into the wastebasket. It sticks to the mitt. He tries to hurl it. Fails. Beginning to panic, he balls the paper between the mitts, runs to the door, opens it, and throws the ball of paper into the hall. A fierce gust of wind blows it back into his room. He repeats the attempt, throwing harder. Same result. The ball of paper lies pulsating with strange vibrations on David's floor. Flinging off the oven mitts, he picks up the object, drops it into a large ashtray, fetches a box of matches from the kitchen cupboard, strikes a match, and tries to set fire to the paper. It refuses to burn. He quickly lights a series of matches, all a fizzle. Mentally regrouping, he picks up the ball of paper, burning his fingers. He carries the ball into the bathroom, locks the bathroom door, unlocks the door,

leaves it open, throws the ball of paper into the toilet bowl, and flushes the toilet. CU of the ball of paper, whirling on the surface of the pool. David repeats the flushing, haggard. The ball has no intention of descending to the infernal regions. David retrieves the ball from the bowl, and dries it. He opens it. Joan's name and phone number . . .

CLOSE UP:

"Joan—216-7089"—shine, more legible than ever.

David: My God.

(Utterly defeated, moving as in a trance of surrender to those reasons of the heart that reason does not know, David removes the goggles and drops them on the floor. He carries the scrap of paper to the desk, and places it beside the telephone, as scripture finding its proper niche in the chapel.)

You were right, Sarah. It's over. No man is an island . . . unless he floods his bedroom. I should have bought a faulty water bed.

CUT TO:

David grimly turning off the Honeywell air conditioner.
MUSIC: *Segue to soap organ.*

David: Goodbye . . . Honey.

CUT TO:

David stuffing rags into the space under the door. With one last look around the room of the (almost) future, David moves to the doors of the balcony. He throws back the drapes. He grasps the doorknob . . .

Hello, cruel world!

He flings open the doors. Polluted air billows in, great clouds of smoke and fumes, obscuring the gallant figure that stands there, resigned, awaiting the end.
SOUND: *With the air pollution, the din of traffic, sirens, jets, crescendo.*
MUSIC: *At first joining the organ, then obliterating it with sheer volume: transistors blaring rock music.*
David turns and, slowly, walks to the telephone, picks up the receiver. Over his dialling Joan's number—CU 216-7089—

CREDITS

The Roncarelli Affair

Mavor Moore

Christopher Grosskurth

Nakash, Montreal

The Roncarelli Affair

Mavor Moore

Derived from the records and reminiscences
and with the collaboration of Frank R. Scott

Characters

TWO WAITERS

BARTENDER

MATRON WITH CHILDREN

TWO BUSINESSMEN

FRANK R. SCOTT, professor of law

PROVOST, LÉVESQUE, BERNARD, BRISSON, and THÉRIEN, inspectors
for the Quebec Liquor Commission

DESROCHES, Bailiff

FRANK RONCARELLI, restaurateur

STENOGRAPHER

REPORTER

HON. C. G. POWER, former federal Cabinet Minister

MME CONSTANCE GARNEAU of the Montreal Civil Liberties Association

A. L. STEIN, lawyer for Mr. Roncarelli

ABEL VINEBERG of the Montreal *Gazette*

PAUL GOUDREAU of the Canadian Press

MAURICE DUPLESSIS, Prime Minister of Quebec

EMERY BEAULIEU, lawyer for Mr. Duplessis

JUDGE MACKINNON

EDOUARD RIVARD of the Quebec Liquor Commission

JUDGE ARCHAMBAULT

FIVE JUSTICES of the Quebec Supreme Court (voices only)

BAILIFF of the Supreme Court of Canada

CHIEF JUSTICE and JUSTICES of the Supreme Court of Canada

ACT ONE

The interior of a first-class Montreal restaurant, small and chic, circa 1946. The main floor, the dining-space, is actually three smaller rooms linked by walls cut away. In one corner, a well-stocked bar. It is midday, and the dining room is filled with its usual fashionable luncheon clientele: a few businessmen, a few couples, and matrons with assorted offspring. Two waiters come and go from the kitchen (in rear), and one barman is on duty. There is a main staircase leading to washrooms and the offices above; a door beneath the main staircase leads to stairs to the cellar, where the wine is kept. The whole atmosphere is one of quiet dignity, unostentatious luxury, gracious living. Customers speak naturally in either French or English, and the waiters are bilingual. There is no musical background.

Waiter: Will there be anything else, madame?

Matron: *(With children)* No thank you, Emile. It was delicious, as always.

Waiter: *(Bowing)* Thank you, madame.

We move to another table: two businessmen are in lively debate.

First Businessman: Il est fou! Il est complètement fou, cet homme-là!

Second Businessman: Duplessis? Pas pire que les autres. *(Making a hooked nose with his finger)* Grâce à Dieu, les politiciens sont tout à fait croches!

First Businessman: *(As waiter approaches)* Ah! une autre bouteille —Châteauneuf, même chose.

Waiter: Oui, monsieur. *(He removes the empty bottle.)*

The polite chit-chat and service continue in the background, while over it we hear the voice of F. R. Scott. SUPERIMPOSE *the date: 4 December 1946.*

F.R.S.: *(Voice over action)* On Friday, December 4, 1946, the well-to-do customers of Frank Roncarelli's popular restaurant on Crescent Street in downtown Montreal were quietly eating lunch. Seconds later they found themselves taking part in a famous case that made Canadian legal history. . . .

Off-screen, the front door slams. Slowly, seriatim, curious customers and waiters look up to see what is going on. Talk dies.

F.R.S.: *(Continuing without a break)* My name is Frank Scott; I was one of the lawyers. This is my voice you hear, but all of us involved in the real events—including my confrère A. L. Stein and myself—are being represented by actors. The play is based on the evidence given at the trial of the case in the Superior Court of Montreal, and on the various judgments in the Quebec Court of Appeal and the Supreme Court of Canada. And the question was: Are the law-makers above the law?

Under his last lines, the waiter arrives with his bottle at the table of the two businessmen. As he raises the bottle to show it to them, a hand enters the picture to arrest the movement. As the shot widens, we see Inspecor Provost of the Quebec Liquor Commission (QLC) seizing the bottle.

First Businessman: Qu'est-il arrivé?

In the main doorway stand four other inspectors: Bernard, Brisson, Lévesque, Thérien, and the Bailiff, Desroches. Lévesque seems to be in charge. They all wear slouch hats, keep their overcoats on, brush snow onto the rug, etc. Shock among the customers as Lévesque speaks.

Lévesque: This is a raid. Calmez-vous, mesdames, messieurs. Please keep your seats. *(To Brisson)* Au bar.

As Brisson crosses to the bar, the Bartender moves swiftly to Lévesque. A mother gathers her offspring to leave immediately.

Bartender: Quebec Liquor Commission?

Lévesque: *(Moving in)* That's right. *(To Bernard)* En dehors. *(To Thérien, as Bernard goes outside to guard the door)* Reste-toi ici. *(To Bartender)* Where's the manager?

Bartender: *(Terrified)* It's Mr. Boala's day off.

Lévesque: Not Boala—Roncarelli.

Desroches, the Bailiff, takes out a paper.

Bartender: Mr. Roncarelli's upstairs, in the office.

Lévesque: *(By the bar)* Where's your licence? It ought to be hanging up there.

Bartender: Oh, Mr. Roncarelli has the licence!

Lévesque: *(To Desroches and Provost)* Allons-y. *(To Bartender, as they go)* No sale—no more liquor. *(Loudly)* This licence is cancelled!

As Lévesque, Desroches, and Provost ascend the stairs, the customers erupt in well-bred anger at the remaining Thérien and Brisson.

Matron: This is a respectable restaurant!

Second Businessman: *(Going up to Thérien)* Qu'est-ce qu'il a fait, ce Roncarelli?

Thérien: *(Shrugging)* Je sais rien, monsieur.

CUT TO:

Roncarelli's private office, upstairs, a small room. A stenographer, at a small desk with typewriter and adding-machine, is totalling bills. Frank Roncarelli (age 42) sits at his own somewhat larger desk, on which lies the day's Montreal Herald.

Roncarelli: What's the total?

Steno: The new kitchen equipment alone comes to nine thousand three hundred and twenty.

A knock on the door.

Roncarelli: Come in.

(Enter Lévesque, Desroches, and Provost.)

Lévesque: *(Muscling Desroches forward)* Faites votre devoir, Monsieur Desroches.

Roncarelli: Can I help you?

Desroches: *(Handling his document)* Frank Roncarelli?

Roncarelli: *(Rising)* Yes.

Desroches: Desroches, Bailiff. *(Gives document to Roncarelli.)* Notice of cancellation of liquor licence.

Roncarelli: Cancellation? I've just renewed it!

Lévesque: Could I see your licence, please? *(Shows badge.)* Lévesque, Quebec Liquor Commission.

Roncarelli: *(Starting to look in desk drawers)* What's all this about? My licence is still good! I sent my application for renewal in last week, with a cheque for twenty-five dollars. What's it all about?

Lévesque: I don't know. I'm only an inspector of the Commission, carrying out my duties.

Roncarelli: *(Still searching)* Where did I put it?

Steno: *(Moving to filing cabinet)* What would it be under, Mr. Roncarelli?

Roncarelli: God knows—look under QLC. We've had it for so long. . . . *(To Lévesque)* Since 1911, first my father, then my mother, now me, we've had a licence, renewed every year. Is it something I've done?

Lévesque: How should *we* know. Maybe *you* know.

Roncarelli: *(Still hunting)* We've never been raided—ever! In over thirty years!

Lévesque: There's always a first time, Mr. Roncarelli.

Roncarelli: Is it some kind of general cancellation? Maybe it's *not* me! *(Sees newspaper on desk.)* Wait a minute. Miss Logan, get me the *Herald* on the phone—I'll find out.

The Steno flicks up the number and starts to dial.

Lévesque: *(Angry)* Now just a moment . . .

Roncarelli: *(To Steno)* City desk. Somebody must know what's going on. *(Keeps hunting.)*

Lévesque: I wouldn't drag in the press, if I were you. *(To Provost)* En bas, Monsieur Provost—faites compter les bouteilles.

Roncarelli: *(As Provost goes)* Now look! . . .

Steno: *(Holding out telephone receiver)* Here's the *Herald*, Mr. Roncarelli.

As Roncarelli speaks on the telephone, Lévesque studies the room and its contents.

Roncarelli: Hello? Listen, this is Frank Roncarelli here. . . . Yeah, the restaurant. Do you know anything about a general cancellation of liquor licences in Montreal? . . . What's so funny? It's no joke—my licence has just been cancelled.

Lévesque exchanges a droll look with Desroches, who shrugs. Roncarelli, listening on the phone, catches Lévesque's eye; Lévesque drops his smile abruptly.

CUT TO:

The main-floor dining room. Customers are leaving, getting hats and coats, making apologies to the Bartender. Provost passes the bar, signals to Brisson, turns to Thérien.

Provost: Okay—en avant!

Thérien opens the front door and signals to Bernard to re-enter. Provost and Brisson have started stashing bottles from the bar into boxes produced from behind the bar.

Provost: *(To Bernard and Thérien)* A la cave.

Bartender: *(Extracting key as he pursues them to the cellar)* No, wait—please! . . .

Provost: *(To the world)* That's all—no more liquor!

CUT TO:

The office upstairs. Roncarelli is off the telephone; he waves the cancellation.

Roncarelli: Then who revokes? Who's responsible for this? Can't somebody tell me? There's been a mistake!

Lévesque: It's on the paper.

Roncarelli: *(Reading)* Archambault?

Lévesque: Sure, the Liquor Commissioner—he's the boss. Now where's that licence? . . . I'm waiting.

Roncarelli: Archambault, is he the one?

Lévesque: The only one.

Roncarelli: *(To Steno)* Get him. Get him on the phone.

Lévesque: *(He and Desroches sit as the Steno dials the number.)* You're at liberty to call.

Roncarelli: *(Hardening, he picks up his own phone and dials a familiar number.)* At liberty, uh? Let's find out about that. I'm calling my lawyer.

Lévesque: You may need him if you can't find that licence.

Roncarelli: *(On phone)* Is Mr. A. L. Stein there? . . . Roncarelli.

Steno: *(Replacing her phone)* Mr. Archambault is out. She says he'll call you back in twenty minutes.

Roncarelli: *(Nods to her grimly, then speaks into his own phone.)* No, never mind. Thank you. *(Hangs up.)* He's gone to lunch!

CUT TO:

The cellar: Thérien is stashing bottles in cartons while Bernard jots down the type of beverage. Thérien calls out only "Wine", "Beer", or "Liquor" and the number of bottles he can handle at a time. The Bartender is remonstrating and trying to make out his own detailed list at the same time.

Bartender: Please! I must know what you're taking! What good are numbers without names?

Bernard: Don't worry, you'll get your money back.

Bartender: You think they're all worth the same?

Bernard: It's the way we always do it. If you don't like it, complain later.

CUT TO:

The office upstairs. Lévesque and Desroches are still waiting patiently, while both Roncarelli and the Steno search for the missing licence.

Lévesque: The licence is supposed to be displayed in your bar, Mr. Roncarelli. If you don't even have it here on the premises . . .

Roncarelli: No one's ever asked for it before; why now?

Lévesque: Because it's cancelled now.

Roncarelli: *(Finding it)* Here's your licence.

Desroches: *(Rising to grab it)* May I? Thank you very much. *(Glances at it; hands it to Lévesque.)*

Lévesque: *(Over this)* That's all we need. Let's go, Desroches. *(They start downstairs.)*

Roncarelli: *(Protesting as he follows them)* There's been some terrible mistake, and you won't give me five minutes to straighten it out . . .

CUT TO:

The main dining room. Brisson and Provost are carrying out boxes through the rear, over the protests of the waiters. Bernard and Thérien emerge from the cellar, also carrying boxes. The place is almost deserted by now—only a half-dozen customers remain, including the two businessmen. Lévesque, Desroches, and Roncarelli descend the stairway.

Roncarelli: What are you trying to do to my place? Years and years to build up, and you destroy it in fifteen minutes!

Lévesque nods to Desroches, who goes out the main door, while the Bartender emerges from the cellar with his list.

Bartender: Mr. Roncarelli, I tried to make a list. . . . I don't know what they've got . . .

Lévesque: There'll be no loss. We treat everybody the same.

Brisson and Thérien return to collect more boxes. First Businessman crosses to Roncarelli.

First Businessman: What's happening, Frank?

Roncarelli: I wish I knew.

Second Businessman: *(To Lévesque)* C'était un des meilleurs restaurants de Montréal!

Lévesque: C'était . . . oui, monsieur.

Three newspaper reporters burst through the front door—two with cameras.

Lévesque: *(To Provost, dryly)* Voici les Marines!

Reporter: Mr. Roncarelli?

Roncarelli: Yes?

Reporter: We're from the *Herald.* *(Indicating the second photographer)* Canadian Press.

Lévesque: No pictures . . . I have orders.

The first photographer takes a shot of the boxes being carried out.

Reporter: Are you the police?

Lévesque: Quebec Liquor Commission.

Second Photographer: Then I'm sorry, Charlie . . . *(He takes a shot of the bar.)*

Lévesque: *(Seizing a bottle and thrusting it at the second photographer)* I wouldn't like to get tough! . . .

Both photographers shoot the action. A musical sting. On the flash of the picture, CUT TO *a newspaper "still" of the same shot: Lévesque thrusting the bottle-weapon into the camera, Roncarelli holding him off.*

WIDEN *quickly to include the headline over the picture:*

Montreal *Gazette*, 7 December 1946

PROVINCE HAD TO CANCEL PERMIT OR
ABET SEDITION—DUPLESSIS

Then DROP *to include start of article:*

Quebec, Dec. 6—To have permitted Frank Roncarelli,
self-styled leader of the Witnesses of Jehovah, to continue
to use funds derived from a privilege granted to him by
the Province of Quebec . . .

F.R.S.: *(Voice over)* Three days later, everyone knew why Frank Roncarelli's licence had been cancelled. It had nothing to do with his restaurant.

TAG *brutally with music.*

GO TO BLACK.

END OF ACT ONE

ACT TWO

The campus of McGill University in Montreal. Autumn. Scott, wearing his academic gown and carrying some books, is crossing a square. He meets and briefly chats with passing students, under the voice-over of F.R.S.

F.R.S.: *(Voice over action)* Aside from having lunched in his restaurant a few times, I knew nothing about Frank Roncarelli until that celebrated raid of December fourth. I was a mere professor of constitutional law at McGill University, and a poet with some reputation for social concern. I wasn't exactly looking for trouble—but this Roncarelli case was only the most recent in a long line of attacks on individual and human rights since the war. *Under his voice,* DISSOLVE *to a half-page newspaper advertisement:*

Montreal *Gazette,* 12 November 1946

FREEDOM . . .
IS *YOUR* AFFAIR
Do these Facts alarm you?

. . . .

Montreal Civil Liberties Assoc.
RALLY at the Monument National
December 12, 1946

F.R.S.: *(Voice over, continuing directly)* About a month earlier, some friends and I—both French- and English-speaking, and of various political persuasions—had formed the Montreal Civil Liberties Association. The Roncarelli incident provided us with our first call to arms. Within the week we mounted a rally to protest the provincial government's action.

During F.R.S.'s narration, we have dissolved from the advertisement to the actual rally in the Monument National. Tight news-film shots of the platform party and the speaker's podium, with the audience area obscured by blinding spotlights. SUPERIMPOSE *legend:*

Le Monument National, Montreal
12 December 1946

CUT TO:

Close-up of the Hon. C. G. Power, former federal Cabinet Minister, identified by a superimposed title. Similarly identify Constance Garneau when she speaks.

Power: . . . In this good province, our Prime Minister, who is also his own Attorney General, has publicly condemned for no less a crime than sedition a fanatical religious sect with whose views few of us have any sympathy, but whose rights to fair trial we all of us maintain. *(Applause.)* We have seen a citizen of this province deprived of his livelihood, merely because in the exercise of his legal right to put up bail for his fellow religionists, he has run counter to the views of a political Attorney General. *(Applause.)*

No opportunity whatsoever was given the accused person to defend himself—and the point I must drive home is that if it can happen to Frank Roncarelli today, it can happen to you to-morrow!

Overwhelming applause. DISSOLVE TO *Mme Constance Garneau at the same podium. She is reading a resolution.*

Garneau: . . . resolu que cette assemblée de citoyens de Montréal sous les auspices de notre groupement, représentant la plus vaste variété des opinions religieuses et politiques . . .

Let her just commence, then FADE *her speech under F.R.S.'s voice over.*

F.R.S.: *(Voice over)* We passed a resolution protesting the arbitrary action of Mr. Duplessis in cancelling the Roncarelli licence, and calling on him to restore it. And we asked him to apply the laws with toleration and justice to all, without regard to distinctions of race, language, or religion. The usual platitudes—though heaven knows we meant them. Along with everyone else, I thought I had made my protest and done my bit. But that was not the way it was to be.

DISSOLVE TO:

Stein's law office. Stein is at his desk, Roncarelli and Scott comfortably seated facing him. The contrast between Scott and Stein, in both physique and manner, is striking: Scott long and cool, Stein short and effervescent. But they have in common a deep social conscience based on profound sanity, and an unmistakable sincerity. They are both reasonable men among a pack of rationalizers.

Stein: Yes, Professor Scott, your part in the rally—but we've approached you for another reason. Your students—and I have one for a clerk—have been spreading the word about your lectures on the relationship of Quebec civil law to British constitutional law.

Scott: *(Smiling modestly)* Ah, I see!

Stein: That's the kind of deep water we seem to be headed for, and I——

Scott: Mr. Stein, before we get onto what lies ahead, I'm not clear yet about the background.

Stein: Well——

Roncarelli: On the way over, Mr. Stein, I filled Professor Scott in on the family restaurant business. . . .

Stein: You tell him about the twelve thousand you spent last year on improvements?

Roncarelli: Yes, and my investments: land, buildings, all that.

Stein: In a few years, *mutatis mutandis*, he would've been making a clear forty thousand.

Roncarelli: Without a licence, Professor Scott . . . *(He shrugs helplessly.)*

Scott: I understand that, Mr. Roncarelli. But of course no one has a *right* to a licence.

Stein: Maybe a legitimate expectation during good behaviour . . . maybe even damages if the cancellation is unreasonable—if it has nothing to do with the restaurant, for example, but seems to be on account of your religion.

Scott: *(Taking the point, rising to move about as he lights his pipe)* May I?

Stein: Please. It's a civil liberty.

Scott: *(Eventually)* I don't know a thing about the Jehovah's Witnesses, except——

Stein: I knew even less. Just at the end of the war, I was down at the courts one day, waiting my turn, when a judge comes up to me and says "Mr. Stein, would you defend this man who has no legal counsel?" Well, sir, in the best legal tradition I replied "Certainly, my lord"—and found myself defending a Jehovah's Witness accused of avoiding military service. He claimed to be a minister, and so exempt from service—they're all ministers, as perhaps you know. Well, I got him off, and soon the Witnesses started calling me whenever they got into trouble—which was often, since the police were hounding them even for standing on the street-corner handing out free leaflets.

Scott: *(Extracting a leaflet from his breast pocket)* Like . . . "Quebec's Burning Hate for God and Christ and Freedom"?

Stein: I thought you said you didn't know a thing about them.

Scott: "Except . . .", I started to say. Someone handed me a copy after the rally.

Roncarelli: *(As Stein glances at him)* It wasn't me.

Stein: *(To Scott)* Well, you and I may take a dim view of the bias, but the facts are true: eight hundred charges laid, over ten thousand dollars in bail . . .

Scott: Maybe, but this is . . . Calling down the wrath of God on the Catholic Church, quoting approvingly a description of the Duplessis government as "a French Catholic Corporate State"— that's pretty powerful stuff in this province. *(Turning to Roncarelli)* You have anything to do with this?

Roncarelli: Nothing.

Scott: You never wrote or distributed tracts like this?

Roncarelli: Never. I have no power.

Stein: He's just another minister, like the rest of them: "When everybody's somebody, then no one's anybody." What he *did* do was to post bail——

Scott: Everyone's legal right . . .

Stein: . . . not only with the court's permission, but sometimes at the court's request.

Roncarelli: Oh yes.

Stein: What's more, every accused he ever went bail for had his case eventually dismissed—every one!

Roncarelli: So I was not even helping lawbreakers, just wrongly accused—until they stopped me posting bail altogether.

Scott: They stopped you? When was that?

Roncarelli: November seventh.

Scott: That was before this was published!

Stein: So for a whole month he hadn't even been posting bail when they lifted his liquor licence on December fourth.

Roncarelli: Sir, I never broke the law, never in my life. Then why this? Why this now?

Scott: *(After a pause, almost to himself)* Inasmuch as ye have done it unto one of the least of these my brethren, ye have done it unto me.

Stein: What?

Roncarelli: St. Matthew, chapter 25.

Stein: *(To Scott)* With respect, sir, can we leave religion out of this and stick to law? Personally I wouldn't care if Mr. Roncarelli was a Whirling Dervish. Someone has done him an injury, and the question is, Professor Scott: who do we sue?

CUT TO:

A conference room in the Provincial Government Buildings, Quebec City. Not a large room: a table with two chairs at one end and space for a dozen chairs facing it. There is no microphone present. About six reporters, male and female, are attending, including Abel Vineberg of the Montreal Gazette *and Paul Goudreau of the Canadian Press. Duplessis and a press secretary are seated at the table. Duplessis has an air of good-humoured shrewdness: a friendly but potentially vicious fox. Here he is being immensely reasonable.* SUPERIMPOSE *legend:*

Quebec City,
13 December 1946

Duplessis: Moi? Ce n'est pas moi, c'est la loi, monsieur. L'article 35 de la loi des liqueurs déclare formellement que la commission peut à sa discrétion annuler un permis en tout temps.

Vineberg: Mr. Prime Minister . . .

Duplessis: En anglais? Okay!

Vineberg: Abel Vineberg, Montreal *Gazette*.

Duplessis: *(Slyly)* Ah oui, c'est anglais!

Vineberg: What *connection* is there, sir, between Roncarelli's membership in the Jehovah's Witnesses and the cancellation of his liquor licence? I mean, had he done anything wrong under the liquor act?

Duplessis: Well, the presumption has always been that the special privilege of selling alcoholic liquor was to go to men of good character, law-abiding citizens in the full sense of the word. We didn't take this action hastily, you know. We studied the matter in its various angles, and reached the conclusion that because he was helping to spread sedition, helping to break municipal by-laws, Roncarelli was not a person to enjoy the privilege which had been given him.

Vineberg: In what way, Mr. Prime Minister, has Roncarelli been spreading sedition?

Duplessis: Oh well . . . he admits he was a leader of this movement, financed by funds derived—mind you!—from what was almost a partnership with the Province! Now this movement is in reality a campaign against public order, you see. People are being pestered in the streets, pursued into their very homes, important people. As Attorney General I would be derelict in my duty if I didn't take means to check what's going on. So . . . *(Indulgently)* . . . this action wasn't directed against Roncarelli because he was Roncarelli. It was against the leader of an illegal movement that we struck.

His final words hang in the air as we CUT TO *the dining room of Roncarelli's Restaurant. Morning. The place is deserted except for a group at one table, drinking coffee: Scott, Stein, Roncarelli. One waiter hovers funereally. Scott and Stein share the Montreal* Gazette. *Open on Roncarelli under Duplessis's last line.*

Roncarelli: Now you know what we're up against, Professor Scott, have you made up your mind?

Scott: *(Lowering paper)* Obviously you've got to sue the Liquor Commissioner.

Stein: But that's not what he——

Scott: His order to cancel is the only hook you have to hang it on.

Stein: I don't think that's what Frank meant. Have you decided to come in with us?

Scott: *(Painfully)* Well, hell, you know I'm behind you . . . but honestly, Stein . . .

Stein: Too busy?

Scott: Not that—it's just that I'm not sure I'm your man. Let me tell you something: Since I was called to the bar twenty years ago, I've never once appeared in court.

Stein: Okay, let me tell you something: I've never sued the Crown, let alone a whole government. We're up to our necks in constitutional law—Quebec's, Canada's, maybe the British Privy Council's—and . . . look, I'm game enough!—but Professor Scott, I'm not as tall as you are.

The dart lands. They both look at Roncarelli, staring glumly at his coffee. A pause.

Scott: *(Softly)* All right.

Stein: Thanks.

Roncarelli: *(Looking up warmly)* Thank you.

Stein: Now: have we got a case?

Scott: Well . . . to sue the Liquor Commissioner personally, you have to get permission from the Chief Justice. You know him?

Stein: Only well enough to know we'd be in a better position with three good lawyers of different political and religious persuasion . . . get rid of those overtones altogether. . . .

Scott: I couldn't agree more. *(Rising)* Let's get at it. *(To Roncarelli)* Where's your phone?

Roncarelli: Upstairs.

Under F.R.S.'s following narration, Scott and Stein accompany Roncarelli as he starts upstairs.

F.R.S. *(Voice over)* And that, roughly speaking, was how I became involved in the Roncarelli affair. But while we got busy, the enemy was hardly idle.

CUT TO:

Duplessis's office, interior. He angrily tosses a pile of leaflets onto the desk, glaring at Goudreau, seated opposite him, notebook in hand. A different Duplessis: no longer genial, but ruthless. SUPER-IMPOSE *legend:*

Quebec City,
14 December 1946

Duplessis: If they want a campaign, they're going to find themselves at war, all right! I'm giving orders to every municipality in the province to enforce by-laws strictly—they've been too lenient. From now on the charge is sedition!

Goudreau: Est-ce que c'est une annonce, monsieur le premier ministre?

Duplessis: Yes, it's an announcement! *(Stingingly)* That's why I'm giving it to you in English, Mr. Canadian Press! Traduction française disponible, comme d'habitude! They talk about liberty —but I'm going to safeguard the liberty of the homes of Quebec citizens. Our police forces have been paralysed by these so-called Witnesses, inspired and led by Communists, and I'm not——

Goudreau: Roncarelli is a Communist?

Duplessis: Hasn't he said so himself?

Goudreau: Well, sir, he hasn't——

Duplessis: We are not attacking any religion or religious belief. We're not depriving anyone of their civil liberties—although I hear more about freedom of the bottle than I do about freedom of the people to live in peace. It's not a question of big government against the little man. This Roncarelli isn't an habitant, he's a very wealthy man. He owns several properties in Montreal alone.

Goudreau: I thought you said he was a Communist.

Duplessis: *(Hitting the roof)* Whatever he is, should the people of Quebec subsidize provocation of the police and flouting of the law? That's not only Communism, it's sedition! We've all seen what happened in the Communist-controlled countries—Russia, Poland, Jugoslavia—and the people have to understand the absolute necessity of combating the Communists, in or out of disguise. And that's a duty we shall not fail in! *(Abruptly relaxing, smiling)* Of course, it isn't true the man had a licence for thirty-five years: he's only forty-two years old! There's nothing vengeful or punitive in this. He defied the law. Don't take my word for it, Goudreau . . . ask the Chief Justice. *(He sits confidently.)*

CUT TO:

Stein's office. Stein is at his desk holding a letter. Scott stands looking over his shoulder. Shaking his head bitterly, Scott walks away, under narration:

F.R.S.: *(Voice over)* Duplessis knew his man. Sure enough, the Chief Justice turned us down—not once but twice. We could not, he said, personally sue the Chairman of the Liquor Commission, Judge Archambault.

Stein: *(Reading angrily)* "In my opinion you have no case!" He's ruling on the merits—when he should only decide whether or not we have a *prima facie* case.

Scott: Imagine! Total destruction of a man's livelihood, unsupported charges of sedition, and he says we have no grounds to go to court!

Stein: Then who do we sue? Either Roncarelli has a case or he hasn't. If he has, there can't be such a huge injustice without somebody being liable. Who do we sue?

Scott: *(After a pause, shrugging)* The Liquor Commission.

Stein: As a body?

Scott: Yes, as a Crown corporation.

Stein: But to sue this Crown corporation you need the consent of the Attorney General.

Scott: That's what I'm suggesting we go after. Just that.

Stein: *(Aghast)* Get permission from Duplessis to sue the Liquor Commission he thinks he controls?

Scott: What've we got to lose? All he can do is say No.

Stein: Yes, but he can take forever saying it.

Scott: Not unless he violates his oath of office as the person obliged to maintain the laws, to look after the interests of the advocates of Quebec. He's a fellow member of the bar, with special——

Stein: He's also a mean politician. I hate to mention it, Professor, but your academic idealism is showing.

Scott: Well, it's better than cynicism. If we assume the whole system's rotten . . . *(Directly)* You want to quit?

Stein: No. You?

Scott: No. What about Roncarelli?

Stein: *(Troubled)* I don't know.

CUT TO:

The restaurant. In the dining room there are only two customers, and they are somewhat embarrassed. The single waiter hovers. The bar is, of course, empty. Roncarelli and the Bartender stand quietly in the hallway.

Bartender: I think I've got a job at Chez Ernest, Mr. Roncarelli.

Roncarelli: You'd better take it, Henry. I don't know how long this can last.

Bartender: *(Helpfully)* It's been a good time, Mr. Roncarelli. . . .

Roncarelli: *(With a weak smile)* Thank you, Henry.

CUT TO:

Stein's office. Stein is at his desk, on the telephone during the narration. He hangs up as Scott enters, removing coat, hat, and overshoes before sitting opposite Stein.

F.R.S.: *(Voice over)* We petitioned the Attorney General to let us sue the Liquor Commission. As the weeks went slowly by, with no response whatever from Premier Duplessis, Roncarelli stood by his case. And on another important front, we had so far drawn a blank.

Stein: *(As Scott enters)* Any luck?

Scott: No. Three more lawyers have bowed out.

Stein: That makes how many you've tried?

Scott: Eleven altogether. One law firm has two million dollars' worth of government business—say they can't risk their client's position.

Stein: Real public-spirited, eh?

Scott: *(Sitting)* I'll tell you exactly what one distinguished colleague said. "Professor Scott"—no, no, he even got so friendly as to call me Frank—"Frank," he says, "in this game you either run with the hares or hunt with the hounds." It seems they're all hunters.

Stein: A nice, homely, rich man's figure of speech! What we need is more poor lawyers. We may yet qualify, my dear colleague.

Scott: Oh, I've got my university salary! It's you who's taking the risks in this affair, Stein.

Stein: Oh, by the way—Professor!—did you remember to renew your membership in the bar?

Scott: Yes, I did. Why?

Stein: It may interest you to know that Duplessis's been poking around to find a way of getting you off his back.

Scott: Good—that means he's worried.

Stein: Worried enough to reply to our letters?

Scott: If nothing else works.

CUT TO:

Duplessis's press-conference room in Quebec City. This time there are a few more reporters, and the Prime Minister makes a proper entrance, nodding and bowing to the press corps. The press secretary sits with Duplessis. SUPERIMPOSE *legend:*

Quebec City,
8 February 1947

Duplessis: *(Donning reading-glasses)* Pour commencer, mesdames, messieurs, je vais vous lire une déclaration en anglais. *(Produces papers and reads.)* "We have received in the past few days a petition presented by the attorney for Frank Roncarelli, restaurateur of Montreal, requesting permission to sue the Quebec Liquor Commission, following the decision to cancel his permit for the sale of alcoholic liquors. This petition has been studied by the legal officers of the Department of the Attorney General, and we have concluded that it is our right and duty to deny such petition. *(His voice fades under narration.)*

F.R.S.: *(Voice over)* And that was how we got Duplessis's reply: not in a letter, but contemptuously in a public press conference. We had to read about it in the papers!

"Roncarelli, by his own account, and there is no doubt on the subject, is one of the leaders of the sect known as Jehovah's Witnesses, whose tactics constitute a danger to public peace, a menace to public order. *(He raises his voice.)*

Duplessis: *(Continuing)* "The liquor permit held by Roncarelli has not been cancelled temporarily but definitely and for all time. Roncarelli is unworthy of benefiting from a privilege given by the Province he has helped to vilify and slander in the most intolerable way." *(Once again, his voice fades under narration.)*

F.R.S. *(Voice over)* But it was then, as we read later, that Duplessis made the astonishing confession which changed the whole course of the case.

Voices: M. le premier ministre . . . Mr. Prime Minister . . . Sir . . . Monsieur . . .

Duplessis: Un instant! Je répondrai aussitôt à vos questions. Un instant . . . *(He raises his voice.)*

Duplessis: *(Continuing to read his declaration)* "It was I myself, in my capacity as Attorney General, responsible for order in this Province, who gave the order to the Liquor Commission to cancel Roncarelli's licence." *(He puts the paper down and smiles.)* Maintenant, chers amis, vos questions!

CUT TO:

Stein's office. Roncarelli sits dourly, Scott is quietly happy, but Stein is positively dancing—with a newspaper.

Stein: He said it! He said it! He said it!

Roncarelli: Nothing he hasn't said before—we're no further ahead.

Scott: No, Stein's quite right: he *has* gone further—maybe too far. The point is, Frank, that Duplessis now admits it was he himself who gave the order to cancel your permit—not Archambault.

Roncarelli: What's the difference?

Stein: Archambault's the Commissioner—he has a legal right to cancel permits. But Duplessis hasn't. It's supposed to be an independent Commission. He's acted illegally, and we can sue.

Roncarelli: But he won't let you sue anybody!

Scott: This time we don't need to ask. He acted outside the powers of his office, and it's just as if he'd been driving round in his private car one night and hit your car. He's liable—we don't need anyone's permission to take action against him.

Stein: *(Suddenly flopping into his chair)* My God, are we out of our minds?

Roncarelli: Yes! Suing Maurice Duplessis, after all he's done to me already?

Stein: *(Picking up the intercom phone on his desk)* Well, he's the one, then, isn't he? *(Into intercom)* Jeanne? Entrez, s'il vous plaît —with your book.

Scott: *(To Roncarelli)* Frank, either we quit now, defeated, or we tie a lifeline to one of the great principles of our constitutional law . . .

Stein: Inherited from Britain, but . . .

Scott: That everyone from the Prime Minister on down is under the law and liable to answer for his wrongs before the courts. The Rule of Law—that's what we call it.

Stein: Okay?

Roncarelli: *(Shrugging)* I'll have to sell the place. . . . But if you men think there's a chance . . .

Stein: My friend, that's all we're ever given in this life.

Stein's secretary enters with her dictation book and pencil.

Scott: *(Dryly, as she passes)* Prenez garde, mademoiselle—the flea is about to attack the elephant!

She smiles back at him as she sits.

GO TO BLACK.

END OF ACT TWO

ACT THREE

A corridor in the Quebec Superior Courthouse for the District of Montreal. Spring, morning. Through the double doors at the end of the corridor march Premier Duplessis and his two lawyers, Beaulieu and Asselin. Duplessis is visibly testy; they talk in low but animated tones. Beaulieu and Asselin are gowned; Duplessis wears a light topcoat and carries his hat. They walk briskly because they know the way well. Policemen, spaced at intervals along the corridor, salute Duplessis, who nods and smiles. All of this under narration. SUPERIMPOSE *legend:*

Superior Court, Montreal,

10 May 1950

F.R.S.: *(Voice over)* It took more than two years for Stein and myself to get Maurice Duplessis into court. On behalf of Frank Roncarelli we were suing Duplessis personally for $118,741— covering loss of the liquor seized in the raid, loss of operating profit for one year, loss from having to sell the restaurant without a licence, and damages to goodwill and reputation. We claimed that Duplessis had acted punitively toward Roncarelli, and without either legal authority or due process of law. His lawyers, led by the distinguished Emery Beaulieu, Q.C., of course denied our allegations.

Duplessis: *(As the group goes into the courtroom)* . . . Et de fait ce sont des menteries!

CUT TO:

The interior of the court. On the bench sits Judge Mackinnon, a solid senior. As the group enters, the clerk whispers to Mackinnon. Stein and Scott are already in place. Roncarelli, Archambault, and Rivard are seated behind them, as witnesses. There are present a few reporters and several armed policemen, but no members of the public except one priest, who takes notes. Under the following narration, those present greet the new arrivals with nods or subdued comment; surprisingly, Duplessis sits not with the other witnesses but with his own counsel.

F.R.S.: *(Voice over)* Duplessis had ordered, quite irregularly, that except for the press the general public were to be excluded from the court. This display of power didn't frighten us, but perhaps it gave aid and comfort to Judge Archambault, the former Liquor Commissioner—the one we hadn't been allowed to sue.

Mackinnon: *(Turning to the litigants, as the clerk leaves him)* I regret to tell the court that we shall have to wait a moment. It seems there is no stenographer available.
General frustration.

Duplessis: But this is . . . this is . . . *(The explosion fizzles as Beaulieu places a hand on his arm.)*
The clerk exits, to return a moment later with the stenographer. Mackinnon studies his papers. The policemen do not hesitate to show their boredom. Stein uses the time to check things with Scott. Roncarelli suspects intentional delay. All this under narration:

F.R.S.: *(Voice over)* Mr. Justice Mackinnon was a federal judge, with security of tenure—not one of those provincial appointments, like the head of the Liquor Commission, who owe their place and their salary to the provincial premier. The trial was naturally conducted in both French and English, depending on the first language of each witness. But most of what you'll see took place in French at the actual trial.

Duplessis: *(Finally rising in umbrage)* Really, My Lord, this is an insult to the Prime Minister of Quebec! There has been a big fire in Rimouski last night, as I'm sure you've read—Rimouski is burning down, as a matter of fact—and there has been another fire in Cabano. I have important provincial business to attend to—and you tell me there is no stenographer!

Mackinnon: *(Gently but firmly)* Mr. Prime Minister, it is the responsibility of the Province of Quebec to provide us with a stenographer. The Court may be federal but unfortunately its staff is not. If you would supply us with more stenographers we would not have delays like this.
The policemen smile. Duplessis is discomfited.

CUT TO:
Rivard on the witness stand. The stenographer and the clerk are now in place; the trial has already commenced. Stein is interrogating the witness. Under F.R.S.'s following narration, the clerk removes the Bible from Rivard's hand pursuant to swearing-in.

F.R.S.: *(Voice over)* When the trial finally got under way, the first witness was Edouard Rivard, who had succeeded Archambault as manager of the Liquor Commission.

Stein: Mr. Rivard, you received a subpoena *duces tecum*, didn't you?

Rivard: Yes sir.

Stein: In which you were asked to bring the Liquor Commission's file on Fránk Roncarelli?

Rivard: Yes sir. *(He holds up a manilla folder, into which he digs for each document as requested, afterwards passing it to the clerk, who gives it briefly to the Judge before adding it to the exhibits.)*

Stein: Would you produce as Exhibit P-1 the licence 68 held by Mr. Roncarelli for the year 1946?

Rivard: I don't think I have that, sir. It should be with the head of the Licence Bureau.

Stein: *(Annoyed)* Well, you do have there the Roncarelli file, don't you?

Rivard: Yes sir.

Stein: Does it contain any reports, charges, or anything connected with the cancellation?

Rivard: I don't think so.

Stein: You don't *think* so.

Rivard: No sir.

Stein: Have you nothing else in the file at all?

Rivard: Oh, I do have *that* here, sir.

Stein: You do have what?

Rivard: The cancelled licence.

Stein: Would you show it, please? *(Then as the licence is passed to the clerk)* Exhibit P-1. *(To Rivard)* Then what?

Rivard: The application for renewal that was denied.

Stein: *(As it is passed to the clerk)* Exhibit P-2. Then what?

Rivard: The report of the inspector who carried out the licence cancellation. *(He flashes a look at Archambault, whose cautious reaction we catch.)*

Stein: Exhibit P-3. What next, Mr. Rivard?

Rivard: The Commission's cheque, payable to F. Roncarelli, for the seized effects less ten percent, the usual . . .

Stein: Exhibit P-4.

Beaulieu: *(Interrupting)* It was cashed, the cheque? *(Rivard nods.)* Endorsed by Roncarelli? *(Glancing at Roncarelli)*

Rivard: Yes . . . the Canadian National Bank, I believe.

Stein: Anything else, Mr. Rivard?

Rivard: That's all I have . . . under my authority.

Stein: That's all you can find in the file on Roncarelli? *(As Rivard hesitates, sharply)* Will you tell the court whether there was anything at all in the file apart from these?—Letters? Reports? . . .

Rivard: No, no correspondence. I have only . . . *(Hesitating)* There is a report from a special officer, dated November thirtieth, 1946. *(He produces it.)*

Stein: *(Abruptly taking it, glancing over it swiftly)* A one-page letter, on Quebec Liquor Commission letterhead, with no signature?

Rivard: Oh, there's a signature. You see?—Y3.
Duplessis looks sharply at Archambault, who winces.

Stein: That's the signature?—but it's unsigned.

Rivard: No, no. You see——

Stein: *(Quickly)* Exhibit P-5. Now, Mr. Rivard, would you tell us: who is this mysterious person indicated by the mark Y3?

Duplessis: *(On his feet instantly)* As Attorney General, I cannot permit that question.

Mackinnon: *(Gently)* Sir, this is not——

Duplessis: *(Undeterred)* He's an informer—I don't mind saying frankly he's a police informer. But under article 332 of the Code of Procedure——

Mackinnon: *(Firmly)* Will the defendant please——

Duplessis: I must inform Your Lordship! Judge Archambault here was the Liquor Commissioner at the time; he's the one to provide the facts. The witness came later; he knows nothing. *(He sits.)*

Mackinnon: I must remind the Attorney General that here he is neither barrister nor counsel, but a witness like any other—and he will speak in answer to questions put, and not otherwise.

CUT TO:

Archambault on the stand, with Stein interrogating him. Archambault is nervous, and looks frequently to Duplessis for silent confirmation that he is saying the right thing.

Stein: Now, Mr. Chief Justice, at the time when you were still Liquor Commissioner, who first drew your attention to Frank Roncarelli's activities as a bondsman for arrested Jehovah's Witnesses?

Archambault: I had an interview with the Crown Attorney, who told me that Mr. Roncarelli, whom I did not know, whom I'd never seen, was furnishing bail on numerous occasions.

Stein: That was when?

Archambault: Towards the end of November, '46.

Stein: And about the same time you learned that Mr. Roncarelli was one of your licensees?

Archambault: Later. The Court Recorder in Montreal, Mr. Paquette, brought it to my attention that Roncarelli—there was a licence in that name—had stood bond for hundreds of these trouble-makers, who were tying up most of the police and congesting the courts.

Stein: Were these charges written or verbal?

Archambault: Oh, verbal. From the Crown Attorney and the Chief Recorder, sir, I do not require affidavits! *(He looks to Duplessis and Beaulieu, who smile approval.)*

Stein: Then did you launch, on your own authority, any inquiry or investigation to check these accusations?

Archambault: *(Smugly)* Oh yes.

Stein: By what means?

Archambault: By means of a secret agent, at my disposal as head of the Liquor Commission.

Stein: The secret agent referred to as Y3?

Archambault: Yes. His work was entirely legitimate—checking on licensees who might, for example, be using the premises for gambling or other rackets . . .

A SHOT *of Scott, appalled at this rationalization.*

Stein: Had you any suspicion that Roncarelli's premises were being used for such purposes?

Archambault: Not those, but——

Stein: When did you first see this unsigned letter of November thirtieth?

Archambault: I'm almost certain it was the same day. He had given me a verbal report, from which I'd jotted down a few notes, in case the Prime Minister . . . *(He defers to Duplessis.)* . . . asked for details. You see, I had already consulted the Prime Minister—

Stein: The Attorney General?

Archambault: Mr. Duplessis—and he had said to me: "Wait till you're absolutely positive it's the same man."

Stein: And this letter verified that the Roncarelli who ran the restaurant was the same person who had furnished bail for all these Jehovah's Witnesses?

Archambault: Yes.

Stein: *(Reading)* It says he was "bondsman for the Faithful to the amount of over $5,000". The Faithful?

Archambault: Oh well, it's an expression: to me it meant the Jehovah's Witnesses.

Stein: Then it goes on: "He was also fined for contempt of court $100." *(As Roncarelli looks up indignantly)* Did you ever try to find out if that was true?

Archambault: I paid no attention to it.

Stein: And the next paragraph: "This grill is known as a place where City Police can get free drinks, and is also known as a Fast-women hang-out." *(He glances at an even more indignant Roncarelli.)* Did you pay no attention to that, either?

Archambault: None at all.

Stein: The only thing you believed, out of all the information in your spy's report, was that Mr. Roncarelli had put up bail for "the Faithful"?

Archambault: Ah! I had, of course, seen various circulars, especially the one called "Quebec's Burning Hate"—a vicious piece of——

Stein: I'm speaking of the allegations contained in this letter. Did you verify any of them?

Archambault: No, because at that moment I decided to cancel his privileges. *(He observes that Scott writes this down.)*

Stein: On the basis of unchecked allegations to which you say you paid no attention—and the pamphlet referred to?

Archambault: "Quebec's Burning Hate", yes sir.

Stein: Did you ever find, in any place in this pamphlet, the name of Roncarelli, or anything to connect him with it?

Archambault: No. *(Again, he notices Scott recording his answer.)*

Beaulieu: *(Interrupting)* Objection! If you're going to use it, introduce it in evidence.

Stein: No, I'll leave that to you . . . *(Nodding to Mackinnon)* . . . with the Court's permission.

Mackinnon: Proceed.

Stein: So on November thirtieth, one week before the raid, *you* decided to cancel the licence, did you?

Archambault: Yes, and so I called the Prime Minister a second time.

CUT TO:

Duplessis in the witness-box. He is self-confident, well-rehearsed, and at his most charming. Stein has plainly been interrogating him with little success; now Duplessis pointedly ignores him and addresses the Judge.

Duplessis: My Lord, this is what happened. At first I didn't know Roncarelli, didn't even know he existed, much less that he was a Jehovah's Witness. In the month of November, Mr. Archambault telephoned me from Montreal, long distance, and told me that Roncarelli—who time and again stood bond in Recorder's Court for these public nuisances, contributed to the paralysis of police activities and the congestion of the courts—that this Roncarelli held a liquor licence. Now a licence, My Lord, is a privilege, not a right. The Alcoholic Liquor Act states: "The Commission may, *at its discretion*, cancel the licence at any time." As Attorney General and Prime Minister of the Province, charged with carrying out the law—having, in fact, received a very clear mandate from the people to see that the law was carried out—I took note of what the Liquor Commissioner said. I told him, "It's a serious matter; are you sure that the Roncarelli who holds a liquor licence is the one involved?" Judge Archambault said he'd find out and let me know. I said to him, "In the meantime I'll take the question under advisement with my legal officers, I'll think about it and turn it over in my mind, and see what ought to be done." A few days later Mr. Archambault phoned me back to assure me he was onto the right Roncarelli. I told him, "Under the circumstances, I consider it my duty as Attorney General and Prime Minister, acting conscientiously in my official capacity—and fulfilling a mandate given me by the people, a mandate renewed in 1948 with an immense majority, *after* the cancellation of the licence please note, and all the pressure put on me as a consequence"—I considered it my duty to tell the Judge that this government could grant no such privilege to an individual with an attitude like Roncarelli's. So that's what I did: I approved the suggestion of the head of the Liquor Commission. And I am proud to have served the administration of justice and the people of Quebec.

Duplessis starts to step down, as if his deposition were now finished. Stein moves in quickly to prevent this. Beaulieu looks at Asselin: the ruse has not worked.

Stein: Mr. Prime Minister, would you tell the court whether it was on *your order* that the Liquor Commissioner, at the time, cancelled the licence of Mr. Roncarelli?

Duplessis: *(Brushing it aside)* I've just said that Mr. Archambault phoned me to bring me abreast of matters, and that after deep consideration I told him I approved his suggestion to cancel. *(He attempts to leave again.)*

Stein: *(Stubbornly)* On what grounds?

Duplessis: *(Showing his annoyance)* Certainly not religion—I know what you're implying. My tolerance in these matters is not at issue, it is a matter of record. No: on grounds that he was one of the leaders of a concerted campaign to disrupt the police and spread sedition in Quebec.

Stein: Were criminal charges to that effect ever laid against him?

Duplessis: No, we let him off more easily.

Stein: Was he charged with any infractions of the Alcoholic Liquors Act?

Duplessis: No, that was not the point. *(As if addressing a pesky child)* I have already told you——

Stein: But what evidence did you have for these other charges, Mr.

Prime Minister? Were they based solely on the two telephone calls from Mr. Archambault, or did you have access to other documentation?

Duplessis: Oh, the phone calls, of course, and an investigation of the situation . . .

Stein: What investigation? *(He glances at Scott, who signals encouragement.)*

Duplessis: It was even discussed by the Cabinet. I consulted our legal advisors, I consulted my own conscience. . . .

Stein: But you accepted Judge Archambault's suggestion without checking any of the facts yourself?

Duplessis: *(Sharply)* I have just told you. I consulted the law, I consulted my own experience. . . . *(Recalling)* And I had received a great many complaints about the nefarious activities of Witnesses like Roncarelli! *(He turns to the Judge, as if to continue.)*

Stein: Did you at any time warn Mr. Roncarelli about these complaints, give him an opportunity to answer the allegations? *(He looks at Roncarelli.)*

Duplessis: *(Pinked)* Surely you're not serious! The Prime Minister of Quebec, a province of 350,000 square miles, a province of——

Mackinnon: You have been asked whether you did or did not get in touch with Mr.——

Duplessis: But that's ridiculous!—Asking *me* to do a thing like that? *(Protesting)* My Lord, must I be sub——

Stein: *(Cutting him off as he produces a clipping)* Mr. Prime Minister, on the eighth of February, 1947, in the newspaper *La Presse*—and I'll make this Exhibit P-28A—there appeared an article entitled "Roncarelli plea denied again". Do you recall it?

Duplessis: *(With forced gallantry)* Ah, sir, you compliment me! I thank you for giving me credit for such a memory, for a power of recall so great I could remember what was published in a particular paper on a particular date, almost four years ago! Despite the compliment, sir, I confess to having no such fabulous memory!

Stein: *(Handing it to him)* Perhaps if you could see it . . . You'll find, Mr. Prime Minister, almost at the end of the story, the following words attributed to you: "It was I myself, in my capacity as

Attorney General, responsible for order in this province, who gave the order to the Liquor Commission to cancel Roncarelli's licence." Now I ask you, Mr. Prime Minister, is this an exact report of your words at that press conference?

Duplessis: What I said at the press conference is what I've just explained. *(Turning to the Judge for understanding)* I didn't know Roncarelli, didn't know he had a licence, until the Commissioner phoned me and filled me in. When he drew my attention to this completely abnormal situation, in which a man benefiting from a privilege granted by the Province was using the profits from it to finance sedition, foment disorder——

Mackinnon: *(Dryly)* It's another question that was put to you, Mr. Prime Minister. *(To Steno.)* Would you read the question?

Steno: *(Reading back from his shorthand tape)* "Now I ask you, Mr. Prime Minister, is this an exact report of your words at the press conference?"

Duplessis: *(His composure cracking increasingly from here on)* What I said to the press . . . was what I was just coming to. This article . . . the text does not conform precisely to what was said. What I said—and I'll repeat it—was that Judge Archambault made me aware of a situation which I, as Attorney General . . .

Stein: What you said earlier, Mr. Prime Minister, was that you only *approved* the suggestion of Mr. Archambault. The words in the article clearly state "It was I myself . . . who gave the order." Now is that report correct?

Scott becomes excited, and Roncarelli even hopeful, as Stein closes in.

Duplessis: The Attorney General of the Province is charged with the administration of the laws, under the Constitution. He is the legal counsel to all government departments. It is therefore completely normal for such officers as the Liquor Commissioner to communicate with him on matters requiring legal advice. And when Judge Archambault asked me about Roncarelli, after having verified his information, I told him "You're in the right: take away the licence, take away the privilege!"

Stein: *(Doggedly)* Are the words used in *La Presse*—"It was I myself . . . who gave the order"—do you believe this is an exact quotation?

Duplessis: I'm not sure what you call it, when the Attorney General, who is the head of a department, speaks to the head of another department, when he gives an opinion. . . . It's not a direct order. If you like, it's an order which isn't an order.

Beaulieu gives Asselin a worried look: their witness is in trouble.

Stein: The question I am putting—perhaps, Mr. Prime Minister, you haven't grasped it yet—is whether you told reporters on that day, "It was I myself . . . who gave the order."

Duplessis: *(Flailing)* What matters is the facts! It happens often during interviews, when you make statements, that ideas aren't translated quite accurately. Myself, when I'm addressing a group I like to establish a rapport, in good faith, to——

Stein: Mr. Prime Minister, forgive me if I repeat the question once again—but this statement appeared not only in *La Presse* but also in other newspapers, and it was repeated in exactly the same form, in both French and English: "It was I myself . . . who gave the order to cancel Roncarelli's licence." Now I ask you again if it is possible you used those very words to the various journalists present?

Duplessis: *(Vaguely, his bravado gone)* These press conferences, you know, sometimes last half an hour, sometimes an hour—and it's difficult for everyone to remember exactly what was said. I can't——

Stein: *(Hard)* Mr. Prime Minister, the truth——

Duplessis: The truth is what I just said, and what I told the journalists, and as Prime Minister and Attorney General I accept the responsibility. If I'd told Judge Archambault, "Don't do it," he probably wouldn't have done it. He made the suggestion and I . . .

Stein: You gave the order?

Duplessis: *(Lamely)* I approved . . . which is the same as giving an order. When a superior officer speaks, the inferior obeys. But I——

Stein: *(Quickly)* Thank you, Mr. Prime Minister. *(Turns away.)*

Duplessis: *(Trying to retrieve the play)* But it was an *indirect* order, in the sense that . . . It's not the same thing . . .

Beaulieu: *(Rising, grimly)* No cross-examination, My Lord.

As a somewhat stunned Duplessis retires, Scott quietly congratulates

Stein. Roncarelli looks from one to the other, bemused. All of this under F.R.S.'s narration:

F.R.S.: *(Voice over)* The rest of the trial, in which we tried to establish damages while they tried to prove Roncarelli had provoked the authorities, was almost an anticlimax. But we had only won the first round.

CUT TO:

Headline:

Montreal *Gazette*
26 May 1950

RONCARELLI WINS
Damages Reduced

F.R.S.: *(Voice over)* Prime Minister Duplessis had no intention of swallowing the insult.

CUT TO:

Duplessis's private office: a TIGHT CLOSE-UP *of Duplessis laughing hugely. We* PULL BACK *to show him standing at his desk, the provincial seal behind him. Facing him across the desk sits Abel Vineberg, the reporter.*

Duplessis: *(Coming out of the laugh)* I wouldn't care if they reduced the damages to one cent, I would not pay that one cent!

Vineberg: Are you going to appeal, Mr. Prime Minister?

Duplessis: As we say in French, "Je n'en connais pas plus que le Pape." Rough translation: "Wouldn't you like to know!" *(He smiles benignly.)*

GO TO BLACK.

END OF ACT THREE

ACT FOUR

Open with a headline, over which we hear the voice of F.R.S.:
Vancouver *Province*

DUPLESSIS WINS APPEAL
—costs to Roncarelli

Quebec, 12 April 1956

F.R.S.: *(Voice over)* It was six years later when we finally got judgment from the Quebec Court of Appeal . . . and we had lost everything.

DISSOLVE:

through the newspaper to the door outside the courtroom. The lettering on the door reads: "Cour du Banc du Roi / (en appel)". Scott, Stein, and Roncarelli are just coming out. The two lawyers carry briefcases. All three are dejected; they walk silently and slowly down a series of corridors on their way out of the building—the voices of the judges ringing in their ears. A few observers look pointedly at them as they pass, but are unacknowledged.

F.R.S.: *(Voice over)* It was a split decision. Four of the five judges were against us.

Justice 1: *(Voice over, echo)* Even if there was an order in the Attorney General's mind, it had no effect unless the Liquor Commissioner had a duty to obey. . . .

Justice 2: *(Voice over, echo)* The Attorney General certainly gave an order, but the Liquor Commissioner had already decided the matter on his own. . . .

Justice 3: *(Voice over, echo)* I can see no order being given, only what might be called an energetic approval in the face of unquestionable provocation by the plaintiff Roncarelli. . . .

Justice 4: *(Voice over, echo)* Even if the Attorney General *had* given an order, he would be within his rights and therefore not liable. . . .

Justice 5: *(Voice over, echo)* The Liquor Commissioner's proposal was not a proper exercise of discretion, and in any case he did not act; it was the Attorney General who acted, and acted illegally.

As the forlorn little group passes through a final door, CUT TO *Duplessis's office. The Prime Minister is shaking hands and slapping backs among a small group of admirers. The chatter, in French, is unintelligible under F.R.S.'s narration:*

F.R.S.: *(Voice over)* There was jubilation in the opposition camp . . . but Stein and I were exhausted and a little bitter. Roncarelli, who would have to pay the costs of the action, was wiped out.

CUT TO:

Stein's office, overlapping the last line of the narration. The three of them silently enter the outer office—a continuation of their exit from

*the courthouse. It is after hours, and the secretary is absent from
her usual place. They remove their hats and light coats, then gravitate
to the inner office and collapse in chairs. Stein offers cigars to the
others, but Roncarelli refuses, and Scott holds up his pipe, which he
proceeds to light.*

Stein: Rinfret had it right, but he was one against four. What more
could he do?

Scott: Still . . . *(Suddenly rising and crossing to a bookcase)* Where's
your Dawson, *Government of Canada?*

Stein: *(Indicating)* Up there, I think. *(To Roncarelli, as Scott
searches)* That provocation theory . . .

Roncarelli: Mr. Justice Martineau's?

Stein: Yes—the theory that you were asking for trouble. . . . *(Shakes
his head bitterly.)*

Roncarelli: Am I right?—He said that because I didn't denounce
the Witnesses I must have been part of a conspiracy?

Stein: The point is that if Duplessis could show you provoked his
action, then he's not legally liable.

Roncarelli: Oh, he'd find some technicality, some trick!

Scott: *(Coming forward, open book in hand)* Here it is. "The judge
stands as guardian to see that the rule of law is maintained; to
ensure that no-one will be punished except for a breach of the
law, and to nullify the acts of any government or government
official which are not legally authorized. The citizen therefore
looks to the courts for the protection of his rights not only against
his fellow citizen, but also against his government and its agents."
*(He replaces the book, but while doing so spots another and takes
it out—under the following.)*

Roncarelli: Words! Sure, it sounds great, but they don't mean . . .
nothing! Lawyers! . . .

Stein: *(Uncomfortably)* Don't damn all trees on account of the dead-
heads.

Roncarelli: Oh, I'm not talking about you fellows—you've been
terrific. I can't even . . . But let's face it, we're licked. Ten years!
Ten lousy years since they raided my place—illegally!—and now
this. I've *had* the law. I can't even pay you for what you——

Stein: *(Gently)* It's all right, Frank, we knew what we were getting into. *(Lamely)* Where they really hung us, you know, was not on the business of who gave the order—we had that down pat—but on whether it was or wasn't part of his official duties.

Roncarelli: What does it matter? If you're big enough you can do anything you like.

Scott: *(Coming forward, another open book in hand)* Not quite, Frank. That's the point: not quite. Listen to this. *(To Stein)* Dicey, *Law of the Constitution*. *(To Roncarelli)* This is British law, but it's what Canadian constitutional law derives from. "Every official, from the Prime Minister down to a constable or a collector of taxes, is under the same responsibility for every act done without legal justification as any other citizen. The Reports abound with cases in which officials have been brought before the courts, and made, *in their personal capacity*, liable to punishment or the payment of damages for acts done in their official character but in excess of their lawful authority." *(He slowly closes the book and pauses.)* Stein, I think we ought to appeal to the Supreme Court of Canada.

Roncarelli: *(Half laughing, half crying)* I've just told you—I'm broke!

Scott: What about the Jehovah's Witnesses?

Stein: No dice. They said if we lost the appeal . . . *(Shrugs.)* Oh, they might finance something further—but not with us—eh, Frank? *(Roncarelli nods.)* They've got a lot of other cases going—it's a small group.

Roncarelli: They tried to get me to change lawyers before. But money aside—what's the use!

Scott: Perhaps I'm just curious. *(Pacing restlessly, he puts the book back on the shelf.)*

Stein: You know what curiosity did to the cat.

Scott: *(More seriously)* But I want to find out, Stein. I want to find out if the Rule of Law really means what it says, or whether it means—as Frank so delicately put it—nothing! *(On the word, he slams a hand down on his briefcase on the table.)*

                                                CLOSE IN:

on the briefcase, under narration:

F.R.S.: *(Voice over)* Stein and I decided it was worth the risk, and

Roncarelli gave us his blessing—which was all he had left to give.
MATCH DISSOLVE:

to the same briefcase two years older, with the same hand on it in the same room. Under F.R.S.'s narration, WIDEN *the shot so that we see Scott lift the briefcase by the handle. He is wearing an overcoat and hat, and walks out of the room followed by Stein.*

F.R.S.: *(Voice over)* Two years later we left Montreal to plead Roncarelli's case before the Supreme Court of Canada.
CUT TO:

The Supreme Court, Ottawa—the second-floor courtroom. At one end of the room, the crescent-shaped bench, elevated, with places for nine Justices. Behind the bench, double doors leading to the Conference Room. In front of the bench, and about six inches below it, sits the Registrar, a barrister. Facing the bench, three rows of tables for the lawyers pleading. Between the tables and the bench, a brass rail demarking an area reserved for Queen's Counsel. Behind the tables, covered benches for other persons, including the public and journalists. The room is less than half-filled.

All nine Justices are present, wearing gowns and tabs. The clerk wears a black gown and tabs. Other court personnel wear gowns but no tabs. An RCMP *constable, circa 1958, stands at the main entrance. The Chief Justice is seated in the middle of the bench, with the other Justices ranged outward in descending order of seniority. At the appellants' table are Stein and Scott, the former sitting, the latter addressing the court. At the respondents' table sit Beaulieu and Asselin. Away at the back, almost in the dark, sits Roncarelli, alone.*
SUPERIMPOSE *the legend:*

Supreme Court of Canada
Ottawa, 2 June 1958

NOTE: *during Scott's address, reaction shots of Stein, Beaulieu, and the various Justices should be taken throughout—and, less frequently, pointed shots of Roncarelli, the forgotten man. Scott speaks from notes, with active assistance from Stein in handing him books and documents from which to quote.*

Scott: This case, Your Lordships, raises grave questions of fundamental freedoms and human rights: namely, freedom of religion and the right to give bail. The learned trial judge found as a fact that the cancellation of Frank Roncarelli's licence was not ordered as a means of enforcing the Alcoholic Liquors Act, but as a punishment of Appellant for having given bonds in the Recorder's Court of Montreal for Witnesses of Jehovah. It was, he says, "indirectly an effort to discipline the Witnesses as a group"— although Respondent failed, in the evidence, to connect Mr. Roncarelli with any provocative activities of that group whatsoever. Furthermore, the learned trial judge stated, "The Court can reach no other conclusion than that the Defendant gave an order to Mr. Archambault to cancel Plaintiff's licence, and that his order was the determining factor." This finding was overruled by the Court of Appeal, but without any manifest error being shown that would justify the overruling.

Now by the Public Law of Quebec, which derives from English law, public officers are personally liable for their delictual acts, whether committed in the exercise of their public functions or outside of them. And the person who orders an illegal act is equally liable with the person who carries it out. In *Smith* v. *Christie*, an action against the Dominion Minister of Agriculture, the learned judges agreed: "The head of a government department, even though a minister of the Crown, may be sued in his individual capacity for a trespass; and this not because of, but in spite of, the fact that he is an officer of the state."

It is therefore a delict for a public officer to usurp a power that does not belong to him, and to act in a manner not authorized by some positive text of law. This is a fundamental principle of the British and Canadian constitutions, the foundation of the supremacy of law over the state and over every state official. The principle is restated by Halsbury thus: "Public authorities, including the Crown, may do nothing but what they are authorized to do by some rule of common law or statute."

Now the Respondent held two public offices: the office of Prime Minister and that of Attorney General. There are no legal powers or immunities attached to the purely political office of Prime Minister—certainly not any right of interference in the administration of the liquor laws of the province, any right to defame citizens or punish them for giving bail. And Respondent has failed throughout to show any provision in the law which gives the Attorney General the authority to cancel a liquor licence.

So the claim on the part of a Minister of the Crown or the

Prime Minister to immunity from suit for personal delict is supported by no authority whatsoever, and is refuted by leading cases and authors throughout the British Commonwealth.

DISSOLVE TO:

Scott crossing the McGill campus. Summer, 1958. He is conversing with two students, a boy and a girl; they are in LONG SHOT *and we do not hear them under F.R.S.'s narration:*

F.R.S.: *(Voice over)* After the Supreme Court hearings, we all returned to our normal rounds to await the judgment. I was deep in a new course on constitutional law—as I told Stein, I'd used up my old lectures in two days in Ottawa. . . .

DISSOLVE:

under narration, to Stein in his own office, in shirtsleeves and energetically on the telephone. Towards the end of F.R.S.'s narration, his secretary enters with a telegram; he signs off the conversation, hangs up, and reads it.

F.R.S.: *(Voice over)* Stein went back to his law practice, trying to make up for lost time, and trying not to worry about what would happen if the judgment went against us. Somehow we'd lost track of Frank Roncarelli. He'd left the province in search of a job, and no one seemed to know where he was when we learned from Ottawa that the Supreme Court was about to deliver the judgment. (X) But by then it was a whole six months later. Thirteen years and one month since they had raided Roncarelli's Restaurant!

CUT TO:

the Supreme Court again at (X) above. This time the Justices make an entrance through the double doors behind the bench, led by the Chief Justice and following in order of seniority. The Registrar and other officials are already in place and standing. It is Monday morning and several judgments are to be delivered; this is, in fact, the first of them. Part of the public area is filled, and this time we are made aware of the presence of reporters, including both Vineberg and Goudreau, both looking older. The proceedings begin with a bailiff opening the Justices' doors and addressing the court.

Bailiff: Order! Order!

The Assembly rises. The Justices take their seats. The Assembly sits. The Chief Justice immediately takes up the first dossier.

Chief Justice: Frank Roncarelli, Appellant, and the Honourable

Maurice Duplessis, Respondent, on appeal from the Court of
Queen's Bench, Appeal Side, Province of Quebec. Held—Justices
Taschereau, Cartwright, and Fauteux dissenting . . .
Brief shots of dissenters.

Chief Justice: No satisfactory reason has been advanced for the
Court of Appeal setting aside the finding of fact by the trial judge
that the Respondent ordered the Quebec Liquor Commission to
cancel the Appellant's licence. By wrongfully and without legal
justification causing the cancellation of the permit, the defendant
became liable for damages under article 1053 of the civil code.
The action should be maintained, and the amount of damages
awarded at trial should be increased by $25,000.

A slow pull-back to a WIDE SHOT, *covering a stir in the court.
We see Vineberg and Goudreau exchange a look, and slowly rise to
file their stories. Others leave. Over this, the Chief Justice starts to
read the next judgment; but we hear only the beginning of it before
his voice is lost in the* CROSS-FADE.

Chief Justice: The Canadian Broadcasting Corporation, Appellant,
and the Attorney General for Ontario, Respondent, on appeal
from the Court of Appeal for Ontario. The Canadian Broadcasting Corporation was charged before a magistrate with violating
the Lord's Day Act by operating a broadcasting station on the
Lord's Day . . .

DISSOLVE TO:

*Duplessis's office. He stands looking out the window, soberly. First
in silhouette, he turns—under F.R.S.'s narration—to his desk, from
which he slowly picks up a copy of the judgment. He sits to study it,
and gradually a confident smile breaks over his face. All of this
under:*

F.R.S.: *(Voice over)* But the motto of Quebeckers is "Je me sou-
viens"—"I remember"—and Duplessis had forgotten nothing.
There was an election coming up, and we heard that he planned
to use the Roncarelli decision of the Supreme Court as another
example of federal interference in the affairs of Quebec. After all,
the majority on the federal bench was both English and Protestant, and he could turn this to good account.

DISSOLVE TO:

F. R. Scott, today, clearly in a television studio; lights and cameras are visible. His voice continues without a break, linking the voice-over narration with the man, whom we now see in person for the first time. He walks a little and then, under the guidance of the floor-manager, sits. SUPERIMPOSE *the date of the actual broadcast.*

F.R.S.: *(On camera)* A few months later, however, Maurice Duplessis was dead. Frank Roncarelli got a construction job in the United States. A. L. Stein became a Queen's Counsel . . . and I went back to my teaching at McGill, from which I've just retired. But this story isn't really about them or us. It's about human rights . . . and the Rule of Law. *La primauté du droit.* Good-night.

GO TO BLACK.

Postscript Notes, Questions, and Projects

How I Met My Husband

Postscript Notes

Rural Ontario, which was Alice Munro's childhood home, provides the setting for most of her works and her major themes. One of these themes is the conflict between a sensitive, innocent young person and a strict, self-righteous society founded on Protestant beliefs of rigid sexual and social morals. Munro suggests that the young person's explorations into herself crack this moralistic veneer, and great effort is made to paint over or cover up this crack in order that the young person be forced to conform. This pattern of conformity and individuality is structured on concepts of guilt that are repressive and uncreative.

A recurring element of Munro's works is the use of a narrator who reminisces about herself while younger. This narrator adds dimensions of maturity and depth, so that we realize that somehow the younger person overcame this conflict; what we concentrate on then is how she managed to overcome it.

In order to survive, the young person must choose between various models or create her own model. There are those who escape from the moral friction, and those who attempt to live within it, those who impose their beliefs in order to convert people, and those who sympathize with young people's struggles while still maintaining their belief in the accepted morality. Still others create the impression that they accept the morality, but they secretly believe otherwise. Yet another part of this moral tapestry are those who commit every sin imaginable while believing they are the holiest of the holy. The models are plentiful, but the choice is difficult and dangerous, particularly for girls and young women.

"How I Met My Husband", a television drama adapted from one of Alice Munro's short stories found in *Something I've Been Meaning To Tell You*, plays out this moral dilemma.

Questions

1. "Chris Watters symbolizes the carefree, casual, restless longing in all of us. He flies over probems rather than meet them. He points out to all he meets that their lives are routine, narrow, and boring.

Small wonder that he fascinates and intrigues women." Analyse this statement in relation to the following:

(i)   Loretta Bird
(ii) Mrs. Peebles
(iii) Alice Kelling

2. In Scene 20 Edie makes two important statements about this television drama's meaning:

> "If there's two kinds of women, one kind waiting and the other kind busy and not waiting, I knew which kind I had to be."

> "Why shouldn't people think what pleases them and makes them happy?"

Explain how these statements relate to the following pairs of characters:

(i) Loretta Bird and Edie
(ii) Alice Kelling and Edie

3. "Act Four, Scene 17, presents a chilling look at a prim and prudish sexuality that explains why violence lurks under a veneer of morality. We see the vengeance of a woman spited, the leer of a busybody, and the desperation of an innocent accused. Chris Watters' escape sets off a chain of reactions that almost destroys two women." Discuss.

4. Discover and research in your library photographic, print, and audio documents on the late 1940s (the time period of "How I Met My Husband"). Audiotape a ten-minute radio program to introduce others in your class to this time period. Videotape a ten-minute program using the photographic documents as your visuals and the print or audio documents as your sound track.

How did the late 1940s in Canada differ from today? Is growing up different today than in those days?

Projects

1. Experiment in groups of two with all the different ways that Scene 2 could be acted out and televised. Develop a storyboard for your television shots. The acting problem is that Edie says nothing while Loretta never stops talking. The television problem is that a wide variety of camera takes must be developed to make the scene interesting to the viewer.

2. Create a storyboard for a three-minute television program on how you did something for the first time. Include what camera takes and audio you would use. Share your storyboards with others in your class.

3. In Scenes 3 and 6, we see Edie fantasizing or playing out her fantasies. Using a cardboard box, magazines, newspapers, and glue, create a "fantasy box" which represents your fantasies, dreams, and hopes. Use both the outside and the inside of the box. Share your fantasy box with other members of the class.

4. Re-read Alice Munro's character sketches at the beginning of "How I Met My Husband". Create your own character sketches for five new people that might be developed into an interesting television drama. Be prepared to outline what might be the first part of such a television drama. Share your character sketches and the beginning of your television drama with others in the class. As a group, create scenarios from the individually created character sketches.
(i) Dramatize them.
(ii) Videotape them.

5. To what extent could Edie be blamed for causing her own situations with Chris Watters and Alice Kelling? Determine whether Edie shapes her own situation or if she is caught up in events beyond her control.

6. Compare Alice Munro's ideas of women in "How I Met My Husband" with those of Hugh Hood in "Friends and Relations" and of Eric Nicol in "The Man from Inner Space".

Friends and Relations

Postscript Notes

The Roman playwright Seneca once said, "When a woman thinks . . . she thinks evil." Rudyard Kipling, the famous British writer, maintained "And a woman is only a woman but a good cigar is a smoke." Napoleon Bonaparte was once moved to say, "What a mad idea to demand equality for women!" But Hugh Hood suggests that it is a "man's world" only because women allow it to be so, and that if they set their minds to it women can be men's equals (if not their superiors).

Hugh Hood's comedy and social criticism are based on two factors: first, stereotypes of quietly suffering women; second, the concept that revenge is sometimes sweet. Far from suggesting that "a woman's place is in the home", Hood presents us with one woman as a model to call into question many assumptions about women's place in society or in business. Our involvement, then, with the difficult but meteoric rise of Mrs. Bird to the highest real-estate peaks arises not only from our sympathy with underdogs, but also from our desire to see people in general, not just women, as masters of their own fates. It is particularly ironic, therefore, that Mrs. Bird gains mastery not only over her seemingly difficult situation of being a widow, but also over the male-dominated society in which she now must earn her living.

Hood also suggests that to be economically successful one cannot be too dependent on one's relatives or friends. Often those who are aggressive in money matters must forget the usual social niceties and family responsibilities. In fact, usually such social values are disadvantageous or are useless in business circles. This kind of success, however, does have its price. The search for economic independence has more to do with ancient survival tactics than with logic or reason. Also, achieving success has nothing whatsoever to do with whether you are a man or a woman—success is dependent only on whether you have the abilities to survive and dominate in a competitive market.

In the end, then, Hood suggests that ambitious men and women must re-think their ties with friends and relations if they are to "make it".

Questions

1. Narrative summarizes drama, while drama expands story. Analyse and discuss how Hugh Hood adapted the short story "Friends and Relations" into a television drama. Be specific about what elements he adapted from the short story.

2. In Scenes 1, 2, and 3, Hugh Hood presents various forms of consolations and reactions people have when someone has died. Examine these to determine what kind of society Hood is portraying.

Pay attention to the dramatic effect of Mrs. Bird's entry and early speeches.

3. Determine to what extent Mrs. Bird's change of character results from the following:
(i)   her new ideas of "friends and relations"
(ii) her desire for independence
(iii) the community's values
(iv) business ethics

4. "Hugh Hood's comedy stems not from Mrs. Bird's reversal of role (this is seen and accounted for early in the play), but from the reactions of her family and friends to her new self. She literally turns them head over heels, sells their property from under their feet and pushes them out of the way with a bulldozer." Discuss whether or not this statement summarizes Hood's comedy.

5. Compare Hugh Hood's ideas of the roles of men and women as presented in "Friends and Relations" with those of Eric Nicol as presented in "The Man from Inner Space" and those of Alice Munro as presented in "How I Met My Husband".

6. Discuss whether or not our society demands that men and women play certain roles. If so, what are those roles? How could one change these role expectations?

7. "Both Hugh Hood and Mrs. Bird are realists—they believe in, and understand, the power of money. They just find others' failure to see the power money can bring very funny." Explain how this statement outlines the dramatic conflict in this television drama.

Projects

1. A "time line" is a method of visualizing periods of time in your life. To create one, collect magazines, newspapers, a clothes line and clothes pegs. Tie the clothes line up in your classroom (it is best to start work on the line by having it three feet from the ground; desks and chairs are good to use as anchors). Do you want your "time line" to be straight, curved, or a special shape? Remember, the "time line" represents your life.

Cut out photographs and printed matter from the magazines and newspapers that represent periods of time in your life. You may also want to include photographs of yourself, your family, or your friends.

Are there any poems or quotations that you believe express what you were at various points of time in your life? Put these on sheets of paper and add them to your photograph and picture collections.

Using the clothes line and pegs, arrange your collection of materials so that the result represents your "time line".

Determine how this "time line" could be made into a play or television drama. Videotape your "time line" into a record of yourself, and your friends and relations.

2. In groups of two, create a collage representing women's rights. Use only photographs, advertisements, and stories from magazines and newspapers.

Select two passages from "Friends and Relations" that could be read aloud while people are viewing your collage. Recorded music could also be used as a background effect for viewers.

3. Redramatize Scene 18, involving Godfrey and the "apotheosis" of Mrs. Bird, but do not use any spoken words. Concentrate on the two people's gestures and facial expressions. Analyse how this scene would be played differently

(i)   on the stage
(ii)   using videotape equipment
(iii)   using storyboards

4. Prepare a one-minute speech on the issue "Parents are more responsible for their children than are children for their parents". In groups of five, hold a panel discussion, with a moderator, on this issue.

The Man from Inner Space

Postscript notes

What will happen to modern man when his social and interpersonal environment (his outer space) becomes so repugnant and intolerable that he can no longer cope with it? Where will he escape to? Will this harsh reality be rejected or will a new, personally created fantasy take its place? Can a sense of humour overcome all problems? Is love all we need? How violent will we become?

A sociologist might answer these questions in one way. A politician might approach them in another. But a satirist will laugh at them all, poke fun at you for asking them, and then show how silly human life really is, if taken seriously. But the catalogue of questions above are some of the very issues that Eric Nicol tackles in this television drama. That he deals with them through humour and wit makes his answers no less important than the sociologist's or the politician's.

Nicol presents us with three complex characters, all of whom represent, in certain ways, solutions to living in cities. One escapes into the private corridors of his inner space. Another searches eagerly for meaningful relations with multitudes of people. The third takes advantage of others to survive. As a result of a seemingly accidental meeting, David learns that his escape into inner space provides no solution at all to his problem. He must learn to get rid of his full-time preoccupation with himself and invest his efforts totally in developing his relations with Joan. This recognition that emotion is very limiting and that feelings for another are the only thing of value is as old as comedy itself.

The satirist must be careful that he does not just ridicule negative things. He needs to point out some positive values that people can acquire or retain to counteract these negative elements. Nicol uses comedy along with his satire to suggest that all we really do need is love, but this love had better be open, honest, and real, rather than escapist, false, and fanciful.

Questions

1. The purpose of satire is to prod society into improving or eradicating social evils by holding them up to ridicule.

There are two basic schools of satire: the Horatian and the Juvenalian. Horatian satire seeks to make us smile at the follies and foibles of society, whereas Juvenalian satire aims at arousing contempt and moral outrage at social vices and stupidities. Between the two extremes of reaction—amused tolerance and unbridled fury—is a reaction and a course of action that the modern satirist suggests is healthy and normal. Analyse Nicol's satire about the following (be specific about what he is satirizing and what he is suggesting as a "norm"):

(i)   the "Cocacolonization of the planet"

(ii) David's use of the film projector, the record player, and television programs

(iii) the Crusaders for Christ rally

(iv) David's idea of "The Stationary Movement"

2. "Nicol's television drama begins with a visual and auditory cityscape that represents the chaotic backdrop against which his various characters play out their fantasies and escapes. Since their outer space is so negative, Nicol's comedy deals with people's efforts to survive, laugh away, or fight this environment so that their inner space is positive."

Discuss this statement in relation to Joan, David, and Robbie.

3. In Act Two, Scene 5, Nicol has David and Joan debate various attitudes to love. Analyse this debate by making two columns (one for David, the other for Joan) to create a balance sheet of their different ideas. Pay attention to their use of symbols, such as Sarah Goldfish, the Bachelor Maid Agency, *Signpost*, music, Paul Newman, and the exercise bicycle.

4. Part of Nicol's satire results from his attack on the idea that sometimes people know what is right but cannot put this into action. Explain this satire by focusing upon Joan's discussions with Robbie and David.

5. Nicol's television drama "The Man from Inner Space" pokes fun at all of television's soap operas, situation comedies, travel shows, detective mysteries, and evening news programs. Identify the similarities and differences between Nicol's television drama and other television programs. Determine if television programming is "the real thing", "inner space", or "escape".

6. Compare and contrast the techniques of escaping used by David in "The Man from Inner Space" and Chris Watters in "How I Met My Husband".

Projects

1. Eric Nicol's cityscape of Vancouver at the beginning of Act One, Scene 1, creates a visual and auditory image of where his television drama takes place. But the cityscape also reflects his attitudes toward the urban problems of high-rise living, noise and air pollution, and lack of privacy.

Create a soundscape and sightscape of the area you live in so that it shows your attitudes to this area. Tape-record the sounds of people and things. Videotape or photograph the area. Catalogue all the natural and human sounds you hear and also at what time you heard them. Indicate also which sounds you find pleasant, unpleasant, or disturbing. Make a list of steps you could take to improve your area's sights and sounds. Does your area honour inner space?

2. Create a two-minute drama involving two friends meeting. One person asks a question to which the other responds in two ways: first, realistically; next, fancifully. Costumes may help with the fanciful way. Analyse and demonstrate how you would record this scene by writing, drawing cartoons, audiotaping, and videotaping. What do these dramas show about our ways of relating to others?

3. Using magazines, newspapers, glue, and scissors, design a one-minute commercial for a product called "Reality" that kills the pain of "Cocacolonization". No person is to appear in the commercial, but you can use voice-over narration. Videotape the commercial.

The Roncarelli Affair

Postscript Notes

What would you do if suddenly, late at night, someone claiming to be the police knocked on your door and demanded entry? How would you protect yourself if you felt that your rights were being violated? What are the differences between rights, privileges, and laws? Do we all mean the same thing when we speak of "justice"? Are officials of the state "above" the law? All of these issues are focused on in "The Roncarelli Affair".

This documentary television drama investigates how three people opposed the seemingly powerful bureaucracy and officialdom of a provincial government—a government whose duty it was to protect the rights of all its citizens, not just certain ones.

Another issue in the drama is the extent to which a person must make sacrifices in order to fight for a principle or belief. "The Roncarelli Affair" suggests that such sacrifices and struggles are necessary if we are to live in a civilized society. But it also maintains that the price for such principles is high.

What defences do citizens of a democracy have against the seemingly all-powerful political apparatus of the state? "The Roncarelli Affair" maintains that those who choose to fight against such power must realize that their opponents can mount an array of supporters (lawyers and bureaucrats) and can often manipulate the media (newspapers, radio, television) for their own purposes. What this television drama does offer those who oppose political suppression is the example of one group of people who kept pressing for the correct and legal interpretation of the law against the state's arbitrary interpretation.

"The Roncarelli Affair" intimates that there is a further agent in society that protects people's rights—the press. Some refer to this agency as the "fourth estate", since it works to present an objective and unpolitical analysis of what happens in government. Notice how Moore and Scott portray its function within their drama. Like the press, the authors suggest that we too must work hard to protect the rights of minorities and our individual freedoms.

Questions

1. In Act Four, F. R. Scott's speech in the Supreme Court explains that in Canada the law is supreme over the state and its officials. Yet, paradoxically, it is the state and its officials that create and maintain that law. Explain how this paradox relates to the following:
(i)   Premier Maurice Duplessis
(ii)   the Quebec Liquor Commission
(iii)   Frank Roncarelli

2. "The Roncarelli Affair", Scott says, is not about Duplessis, or Roncarelli, or even Scott; it is about human rights and the Rule of Law. Analyse whether or not we, as readers or viewers, should be more concerned with the abstract than with the particular, with the concept than with the actual. In what historical or present events is this issue of rights and the Rule of Law relevant?

3. "The Roncarelli Affair" presents a complex view of Premier Duplessis as a politician. Determine his values in relation to the following:
(i)   Jehovah's Witnesses

(ii)   journalists and the press
(iii) the Francophone/Anglophone problems in Quebec
(iv)   political patronage

4. "The Roncarelli Affair" is a documentary television drama. Analyse and explain the effectiveness of the following elements:
(i)   the use of newspaper headlines
(ii)   the voice-over narration of F. R. Scott
(iii) the use of dialogue from trial transcripts
(iv)   the ending

5. Determine if societies or communities could exist without laws. Must a society have defenders of the laws as well as those who defend people against the laws?

6. Both "The Roncarelli Affair" and Nicol's "The Man from Inner Space" provide social commentaries on living in Canada. Compare and contrast the following issues as presented in these two television dramas:
(i)   the relations between individual freedom and social law
(ii)   the responsibilities each person has to other people

Projects

1. Obtain and analyse a copy of Canada's Bill of Rights. Using newspapers and magazines, document with pictures and print material that these rights exist for Canadians. Using part of F. R. Scott's speech in the Supreme Court (Act Four) as a sound track, create a presentation that explains what Canada's Bill of Rights means to us.

2. Create ten questions that could be used in a survey to determine people's attitudes towards freedom and the law. Survey at least ten different people with the questions and record your results in writing, or with audio or video tape-recorders. If possible, survey a lawyer and a member of the police. Analyse how your survey results reflect on the issues found in "The Roncarelli Affair".

3. In your library, research the important events during Premier Duplessis's years of power in Quebec. Create a display board that outlines these events. From this research, create a sound track for your display on a tape-recorder, so that others can hear of these events while viewing the display.

4. List as many instances as possible that you and your class can think of in which your individual freedom has been limited by laws or rules. Select several of these instances for dramatization in which the solutions are left to the viewer. Determine as a class what the solutions might be. Audiotape or videotape both the dramatizations and the solutions.

5. Using newspapers and magazines, collect photographs and print materials that illustrate the relation between freedom and the law. Create a collage from these materials that represents this theme. Compare your collage with those of others. Determine how these collages could best be visually presented through videotaping.

Bibliography

Bibliography

Alice Munro

Dance of the Happy Shades. Ryerson Press (Toronto, 1968).
Lives of Girls and Women. McGraw-Hill Ryerson (Toronto, 1971).
Something I've Been Meaning To Tell You. McGraw-Hill Ryerson (Toronto, 1974).

Articles, Criticism

Frank Davey. Article on Alice Munro's writings, in *From There to Here: A Guide to English-Canadian Literature Since 1960.* Press Porcépic (Erin, 1974), pp. 201–4.

Graeme Gibson. Interview with Alice Munro, in his *Eleven Canadian Novelists.* House of Anansi (Toronto, 1973), pp. 241–64.

John Metcalf. "A Conversation with Alice Munro", *Journal of Canadian Fiction* I:4 (1972), pp. 54–62.

Clara Thomas. Review of *Lives of Girls and Women, Journal of Canadian Fiction* I:4 (1972), pp. 95–6.

Hugh Hood

Flying a Red Kite. Ryerson Press (Toronto, 1962).
White Figure, White Ground. Ryerson Press (Toronto, 1964).
Around the Mountain. Peter Martin Associates (Toronto, 1967).
The Fruit Man, The Meat Man and The Manager. Oberon Press (Ottawa, 1971).
You Can't Get There from Here. Oberon Press (Ottawa, 1972).

Articles, Criticism

Pierre Cloutier. "An Interview with Hugh Hood", *Journal of Canadian Fiction* II:1 (Winter, 1973), pp. 49–52.

Frank Davey. Article on Hugh Hood's writings, in *From There to Here: A Guide to English-Canadian Literature Since 1960.* Press Porcépic (Erin, 1974), pp. 138–42.

Eric Nicol

Beware the Quickly Who. Playwrights Co-op (Toronto, 1967).

The Clam Made a Face: A Play for Children. New Press (Toronto, 1972).

The Fourth Monkey. Talonbooks (Vancouver, 1973).

Girdle Me a Globe. McGraw (Toronto, 1957).

Shall We Join the Ladies? Paperjacks (Don Mills, 1973).

Collaborations

with Peter Whalley. *Russia Anyone? A Completely Uncalled-For History of the U.S.S.R.* McGraw-Hill (Toronto, 1963).

F. R. Scott

The Canadian Constitution and Human Rights. Canadian Broadcasting Corporation (Toronto, 1959).

Selected Poems. Oxford University Press (Toronto, 1966).

Collaborations

with A. J. M. Smith (ed.), *The Blasted Pine: An Anthology of Satire, Invective and Disrespectful Verse, Chiefly by Canadian Writers.* Macmillan of Canada (Toronto, 1957; 1960 [paperback]).

Articles, Criticism

Desmond Pacey. "F. R. Scott", in his *Ten Canadian Poets.* Ryerson Press (Toronto, 1958).

A. J. M. Smith. "F. R. Scott and Some of His Poems", *Canadian Literature*, 31 (Winter, 1967), pp. 25–35.

Peter Stevens. *The McGill Movement.* The Critical Analysis Series. Ryerson Press (Toronto, 1969).

Clara Thomas. Article on F. R. Scott's writings, in *Our Nature—Our Voices: A Guidebook to English-Canadian Literature*, vol. 1. New Press (Toronto, 1972), pp. 106–9.

Videotaping

Tony Gibson. *The Practice of ETV*. Hutchinson Educational Ltd. (Toronto, 1970).

————. *The Use of ETV*. Hutchinson Educational Ltd. (Toronto, 1970).

Jim Moriarty. *The Third Eye*. Ontario Educational Communications Authority (Toronto, 1972).*

———— and Jack Livesley. *Behind the Third Eye*. Ontario Educational Communications Authority (Toronto, 1973).*

*Direct inquiries to the Utilization Section, O.E.C.A., 2180 Yonge Street, Toronto, Ontario. M4T 2T1.

67 77 87 97 08 18 28 38 48 THB 9 8 7 6 5 4 3 2 1